WITCHCRAFT
PAST AND PRESENT

WITCHCRAFT PAST AND PRESENT
for the Millions

Marika Kriss

FOR THE MILLIONS SERIES

SHERBOURNE PRESS, INC.　　　LOS ANGELES

Copyright © 1970 by Sherbourne Press, Inc.

All rights reserved. No portion of this book may be reproduced by any means or for any purpose without prior written consent from publisher, except in the case of a reviewer who may quote brief passages in connection with a review. Address all inquiries to Rights & Permissions Dept., Sherbourne Press, Inc., 1640 So. La Cienega Blvd., Los Angeles, Ca. 90035

Library of Congress Catalog Card Number 70-99873

Manufactured in the United States of America by Kingsport Press, Inc., Kingsport, Tenn.

Second Printing
SBN 0-8202-0019-0

CONTENTS

Preface	WITCHES!	7
Chapter One	FLYING BACKWARDS THROUGH TIME	13
Chapter Two	THE CHURCH AS WITCH	21
Chapter Three	SADISM	29
Chapter Four	COVENS AND SABBATS	42
Chapter Five	WHERE WITCHES LIVE	57
Chapter Six	THE LADY OF WITCHES	71
Chapter Seven	HEALING AND BLIGHTING	81
Chapter Eight	THE EVIL EYE	93
Chapter Nine	EL BRUJO	103
Chapter Ten	VESTIGIAL WITCHCRAFT AND NEW GROWTH	114
Chapter Eleven	HIPPIE WITCH	141
Chapter Twelve	BEGINNINGS	159

PREFACE

Witches!

When we learn the word *witch* as youngsters, it usually comes complete with a disclaimer. "Nowadays, of course, we know witches don't really exist. They are a superstition. Or they are a game we play on Halloween."

However, today as always, those who do not believe in witches represent an exceedingly small proportion of the earth's population. And if that population were expanded to include all the humans who walk or have walked under the stars, the proportion of disbelievers would shrink to less than one percent.

The truth of the matter is that there *have been* witches and there *are* witches. What we do not know is the parameters of the craft. Is the magic in witchcraft sleight-of-hand or truly occult? Are witches normal human beings who have been molded by a specialized educational process? Are they supernormal? Are they subnormal? Or are they normal in most respects, but with a scattering of wild talents such as extrasensory perception? Are they evil? Or are they beyond evil?

This book does not pretend to answer these questions, but does hope to prepare the way for an eventual answer by offering a consideration of our ancestral witches, the flourishing sorcery that is accessible to us for further observation, and the witchcraft that is currently being practiced in the hostile environment of Western civilization.

The usual discussion of witchcraft makes a production of attempting to pinpoint the moment when such wish-fulfilling superstition first invaded European life. Then it goes on to describe the spread of witchcraft, the various factors which influenced its practice, and the attacks leveled against it by secular and ecclesiastical governments and segments of the lay population.

This is done with the air of a medical historian seeking to establish the time and place syphilis was introduced into Europe, its dispersion, and the subsequent attempts to scourge the disease from the land. Further, it is customary to think of witchcraft, like the dancing madness, as an aberration of the Middle Ages (referred to in this context as the Dark Ages) which lingered into the eighteenth century, a spiritual malaise with no real prior or antecedent existence.

Disregarding the tone of such discussions, this approach is absurd. In Europe, as in the other places early man had to scrounge out a home in a world not willing to make a place for him, witches played a vital part in the effort to stay alive.

What, then, is a witch?

A witch is a person who is able to manipulate the natural world by means of supernatural abilities or tools. Or, to phrase it for the skeptics, he is a person whom the members of his community believe to be able to so manipulate the natural world.

Among the relevant academic disciplines, there is a

good deal of amiable wrangling about the niceties involved in distinguishing a witch from a shaman from a priest. Supernatural powers may be accepted as coming from a god or goddess who, being duly propitiated, is kindly or barteringly disposed. Or such powers may come from a manipulation of the spirit world, which responds to the correct rite correctly performed with an almost will-less mechanical efficiency. Or the powers may come from within the person himself or from the tools he applies. The first, by definition, leans the practitioner toward the priest, the next toward the shaman, the third toward the true witch.

Witches themselves are not troubled by such semantic difficulties. They seize their talents where they find them and apply them gratefully.

Similarly, they are not much interested in the literary distinctions between wizard, sorcerer, magician, seer, warlock, wiseman, and conjuror. They have been known by many names in many languages. It has always been the function that counts. And the function can be performed by either sex, depending on the vagaries of local custom. The only important bit of terminology is their magical names, and these are secret.

The early witches were leaders of their communities. They dealt with its basic concerns: birth, health, death, the welfare of its people, the fertility of the fields and flocks, weather, and the success of its hunters and warriors. Supernatural is the word outsiders use to describe their methods. The sorcerers were keenly aware that their talents were not common. But they were kept humble by the fact that no one of them possessed the entire range of the craft's abilities. Each man had his own specialty or his own combination of excellences.

Witches are thought of as occultists with their eyes

focused on unseeable mysteries. "Naturalists" would be a better word for them. They have always loved nature, feared her, studied her, coaxed and bullied her. They are able to perceive the personality within each natural object and phenomenon, and by addressing themselves to that personality, they are able to obtain responses. A witch was always the one in the community who had a nose for weather, an eye for subtle differences in plant and animal life, and a deep sense of the rhythmic relationship between the communities of living things.

The horns and animal masks they wore ceremonially proclaimed their sense of membership in the animal kingdom. The Christians gradually developed a repugnance for their animal heritage that worsened as they denied more and more of their instinctual nature, until by the Victorian Age it had become a full-fledged phobia. It was the reverse with the witches. They reverenced and drew strength and comfort from their common heritage with other life forms. Emphasizing this heritage made man feel less alone under the stars and made him realize that some of the blueprints for living were coded within his flesh.

Part of the witches' power stemmed from their ability to lose their personal identities in race consciousness as a man, as an animal, as a living creature; to glory in it, to be fulfilled by it, and as a consequence, to accept joyously what life offers. To this end they sought out and adapted for their purposes every natural hallucinogenic the earth offers. They used them during their own training to help unlock the secrets of nature. They gave them to their people during the sabbats, together with the use of timpani, music, chanting, and dancing, to enable their people to let go of personal problems for an evening, a few days, a week, and merge into a sense of oneness with the universe.

The witches were ecologists. They understood that man must live in balance with nature and the vitality they perceived underlying nature. Much of their magic was (and still is) directed to that end. They observed that man's personality, as well as his health, is affected by the life around him, just as both personality and health are influenced by climate, soil, and water. Astrology was born of sorcery, and many witches have watched the skies for the influence of the sun and the planets, the stars and the glowing moon on the affairs of men.

Perhaps as an adjunct to their ability to submerge themselves into other life forms, perhaps as a special talent in itself, the witches felt the emotions of others and were even able to receive flashes of mental imagery. At times their minds seemed capable of jumping into the future and bringing pieces of it back with them. At times their bodies seemed able to soar through space and even to haul passengers or luggage.

Whatever the singularity or combination of sources from which they took their powers, the witches were not content to manipulate the unseen world. They also made use of whatever natural procedures were available and did the job. They studied the rhythms of their own bodies and achieved amazing control over their functions. They developed disciplines which enabled them to slow or speed heart action, withdraw awareness from parts of the body, resist injury, speed healing, and control the tides of emotion. They began pharmacology, surgery, obstetrics, orthopedics, and dentistry for man and beast, and a functional kind of psychiatry that produced results.

The line between the occult and the real that we have been taught to draw, they did not. Not that they were incapable of distinguishing between the type of vision we use to watch a football game and second sight; but to them the occult was as natural as a potato. Both were to be exploited in the day-to-day struggle of living. A witch is a person who, given individual variations in competency, can exploit both.

CHAPTER ONE

Flying Backwards through Time

The craft is one of the earliest specialties mankind developed. Cynics may cavil about the reasons, but the fact of its usefulness is indisputable. Witchcraft is no fad or whim. Its presence is as world-wide as the institution of the family. It is safer to bet that without witches Europe would have been uninhabited than to suppose that the early Europeans existed without witchcraft.

The headman's role as leader did not hinder him from performing the day-to-day tasks of hunting, herding, or farming. The witch, on the other hand, required time for his unique work. He had to search for herbs and roots, brew his potions, perform his lengthy rites gesture-, word-, and tone-perfect, fashion his masks, concoct and apply his body paint, tend the sick, make powerful the hunting and working tools of his people, and, hopefully, see far enough into the future to prevent catastrophe.

When the environment was abundant enough to permit it, his fellow tribesmen took over part or all of the burden of supporting him and his family in return for his full-time concentration on his duties. This is the most eloquent possible answer to the contemporary assessment of their powers. Witches were mankind's first professionals.

Properly, the search to discover the beginnings of witchcraft belongs to the archeologist, not the historian. Unfortunately, the accoutrements of the profession are more fragile than arrowheads. Shards of pots used to make magical brews look much like shards from pots used for cooking stew. Chants, the symbology or design, rites, and above all the aura of supernatural power cannot be fossilized. In the main, we have only paintings on cave walls and an occasional untoylike doll to confirm our guess that witches walked the lands in the paleolithic age, bringing game within arrow-reach, healing the sick, and wreaking havoc on the tribe's enemies.

These are indispensable services. They go hand in hand with the need for food, the danger of falling sick, and the threat of being overwhelmed by the relentless pressure from neighboring foes. The desperate need early man must have felt as an upstart form thrusting his way into a world still populated by giant lizards leads us to suspect that prototype witches were working their wonders among men who had not yet become sapient.

During historic times, the European farmlands have been a constant enticement to peoples whose native lands were more crowded or less fruitful. There has been a steady filtering in of strangers through immigration, and periodic gushes of new blood have followed in the wake of conquest.

Normally, the successful, well-entrenched professional witch stayed in his homeland. However, the old displaced witch, the unproven witch, the amateur, and a few top-notch but reckless witches welcomed fresh opportunity.

At the same time, traders and warriors who had gone out to strange lands returned home with bits and pieces of alien sorcery—perhaps only a talisman or the dregs of a potion, or perhaps, if they were good at making friends, detailed methodology. Often on their return they functioned as part-time witches.

Of course, each local community had its own resident conjurer, and each district had at least one unusually talented witch. And there would be village gossip about a superwitch who lived a greater distance away.

The confrontation between local and foreign witchcraft invariably resulted in a clash of hostility. To some extent, this was a natural manifestation of xenophobia, the fear of strangeness to which the human animal is so particularly vulnerable. Much of the antagonism, however, was the by-product of a power struggle between jealous professionals.

The newcomer had the advantage of appearing exotic and of having no record with the locals as botching one of his spells. On the other hand, the resident was known to his neighbors and knew them, spoke their language, had past experience in coping with their personalities, and had helped them all at one time or another. He was in a position to propagandize effectively.

The classic tactics of the ensuing struggle were for the newcomer to impute ineptitude or secondary talent to his opponent and for the defender to imply that the newcomer was up to no good and that behind the mask of good intentions lay malevolent ends.

From the reaches of time, a record of such a duel has been left behind. It was painted on the walls of a cave, the so-called Dead Man's Cave, in Lascaux in southwestern France. The men who applied the pigment died sometime in the upper paleolithic period. The strange, beautifully fashioned figures they created represent a fight between two witches. In the battle of sorcery one of the contestants had assumed the shape of a bison and was charging his enemy. The other had a human body and a beaked head. He carried a wand on which a bird, his spirit helper, perched ready to throw himself at the oncoming attacker. The painting has no ending. As a rule the defender won. Even without the handicap of being a stranger, the most benign witch provokes in the non-professional an awe that is only half a step from distrust and hatred.

Actually, this reaction is not to the aura of the occult, but to power. Presidents, policemen, referees, heads of the boards of conglomerates, and school teachers can if they wish withhold what they have promised to provide and substitute for the good services of their role great harm. Generally, they are cursed as often as praised, and not uncommonly they are hated.

Witches, like others enjoying the possession of power, encourage awe in their clientele as an additional power source. And always there are those who give in to the temptation to live off community fear, receiving more than they give and loving power in itself. Witches who came into a territory following the sword of a conqueror would inevitably be seen by the locals as (and would almost always be) despots.

Usually, such a community came to refer to the intruders by a label different from their local name for witch. Sometimes they used the name for witch in the stranger's tongue. Sometimes they used the word in their own language for a rogue witch. Along with such name-calling, members of the community often clamored for the suppression of the sinister force. These outcries for succor and the new terms used are the evidence on which casual historians have based their statements that witchcraft was a new phenomenon intruding into the locality.

Actually, what was occurring was a specialization of services. Originally, when a people numbered only as many as could comfortably travel in a hunting and gathering band, they would possess a single all-purpose witch to do the band's blessing and cursing. As the population count grew, so did the number of witches. Certain personalities are better at cursing than at blessing. So conjurers who may have also known a good deal of beneficent magic were hired, due to circumstances, to spend most of their time weakening the enemies of the tribe. By the time the culture reached the status of a kingdom, there were apt to be individual witches who felt no loyalty to the government working as a guerrilla force to subvert the power structure, or as malcontents willing to hire out to anyone to do anything.

To illustrate the process by which local witchcraft was influenced by population shifts, let us consider the consequences of the Roman invasion of Europe.

By the time the legions began marching north, Roman witchcraft had become a cosmopolitan practice. Upon the original, rich Mediterranean tradition had been grafted additions from Egypt, Persia, Crete, the Judaic countries, and the Orient. Without question Roman sorcery gained in scope and power from the influx. Unfortunately, it lost in stability. This manifested itself both in the witches themselves and their patrons. The rift between the two groups became so great that, in order to maintain a class of professionals

17

they could trust to perform magic, the buyers of magical help dichotomized the destructive witch and the magician to whom they went for aid. The very act of doing this further antagonized the witches who were, or were thought to be, engaged in anti-Roman activities.

The amount of fear that must have prevailed among the Romans to force such a schism is shown by the fact that the Romans generally saw life as a unity, not as a dichotomy of good and evil. They had no hope of perfection in this life or the next. Their religion contained no god of evil, no devil, but gods and goddesses who were benevolent or dire in their relationship to man and to each other as the whim took them.

Within the nascent tradition of the evil witch, the Romans feared most the sinister sorceresses of Thessaly, who delighted in homicide by poison and knew and practiced enchantments transforming people into animal form.

During the spring rut and on other designated occasions, Roman witches came from great distances to gather for festivities on the night of the full moon and to perform some of their most powerful feats of magic. Goats were sacrificed, their hides taken and cut into strips. The strips were braided into whips that were used to flog women until the blood streamed down their backs in a ritual of purification by pain. Grudges were paid off at this time by formulas of enchantment, rivals in love were rendered impotent, poisons and aphrodisiacs were brewed. Some wearing the shaggy skins of goats, some hidden behind intricately carved and painted masks, some naked, the witches chanted and danced and, in the heat of the ceremony, howled in the moonlight.

These traditions, including that of the well-delineated evil sorceress, reached northern Europe in the wake of the victorious soldiers. There the witches' headdresses were fashioned from stag horns, antlers, the horns of wild bulls, the cured heads of bears, the carved likenesses of mythological animals. They led their people in ecstatic ceremonies designed to increase the harvest, promote health and sanity, and create a harmony between humans and the supernatural world. Many taught their people ritual cannibalism, which was practised as a communion of the living with the spirit who had occupied the flesh being eaten. Knowledge and customs from many sources mingled. The tradition and the numbers of cursing witches grew.

In a similar fashion, the Angles, the Saxons, and the Gauls, when they came conquering, brought with them their potions and campfire stories, some of which were absorbed into the local craft and some of which gradually died out. They also brought their own witches to terrorize the natives and displace their sorcerers.

In the ensuing decades, feudalism in Europe expanded and altered. Chronic fighting broke out between great lords and their retainers over land which was in increasingly short supply. The crusades sent immense numbers of men across Europe to Jerusalem. The Black Death swept across the continent and the British Isles, creating such a drastic manpower shortage that scions of peasant families chained to the soil for generations were free to travel across the country in search of better returns for their labor. One result of these events was a mixing of local customs and the infusion of magical arts and sorcerers from the Ottoman Empire, the Byzantine Empire, Arabia, Africa, and the Orient.

By the sixteenth century, every city and town in Europe, and many small villages, contained witches of differing backgrounds and differing loyalties within a population that had suddenly grown heterogeneous as compared to that of a decade or two before. This sense of strangeness upon strangeness created spiritual tension in a period racked with secular tensions as well.

CHAPTER TWO

The Church as Witch

Witches came before priests; and spirits—or at least man's recognition of them—came before gods. So the early witches were a godless sort, drawing the skills and strength of their profession from themselves and from their ability to perceive through the outer husk of form the spirit animating an object.

They saw this animism in multitudinous forms: in trees, in the sky, in a spear, in the ground, in the wild grains, in animals, in a pebble, a leaf, a thunderstorm. Whether these spirits "actually" exist is not a matter to debate here. Living witches say they exist; they see them. They talk to them. If we point out that *we* do not see them, we have only restated to them the obvious fact that we are not witches. If we wish to understand witches, we must learn their language and accept the geography of their world.

Some spirits were observed to have more power, more attributes, more personality than others. In this way the witches became the first priests. They discovered the gods: the sun god, the moon, the great earth mother; later there were others.

The gods proliferated; their servants quickened and multiplied. There were witch-priests and priest-witches, priests who practiced a little magic and witches who loved and worshipped the gods. The gods developed a spirit of competitiveness, their followers a tendency to boast, "My god is stronger than your god"; in the main, among the agricultural religions, there was a great spirit of inclusion, a willingness to fit a new god in among the old. Exceptions showed up from time to time; the God of the Jews was a jealous god. However, since his interest was exclusively directed toward the Jews, that was their problem. The God of the Christians was equally jealous, however, and he was an empire-builder. Or at least the church that was organized in his name and multiplied like yeast in the soil of Europe built an empire.

The early Christians were persecuted by the Romans not because they loved and worshipped Christ but because they refused to worship also the Roman gods. The Romans would gladly have included Christ in their pantheon of the supernatural and, had the Christians been less stubborn, would soon have built a temple in his honor. However, they felt they could not afford to harbor in their midst persons who, recklessly committed to an insane policy of inciting the wrath of other powerful gods and goddesses, would provoke a terrible revenge on the entire community. In the end, Christ proved a better god of war than Mars and the Christians better organizers than the Roman emperors. Christianity took the Mediterranean world, pierced northward to Constantinople, and swept across Europe, taking kingdom after kingdom.

While the church was busy fighting its war of deicide

and establishing its suzerainty over the kingdoms of Europe, it ignored the witches. It had, however, begun to steal their act.

In the beginning, Christianity had been directed exclusively toward the salvation of the soul through the acceptance of God, baptism, love of fellow Christians, and purity. Materialism, including the enjoyment of the body, was to be put aside in favor of full-time worship. Such miracles of healing and providing as Christ and his disciples performed were done to certify their authenticity, not as examples to be emulated.

The church had acquired its territory initially by the beautifully effective means of converting emperors and kings. These converts could and did dictate the behavior of their subjects, although they could not compel their hearts. The church then began boring into the hearts of the common men by encroaching upon such practical matters of life on earth as individual health, the fruitfulness of fields, flocks, and the goodwife's own womb, calm seas and wet skies, favor in love, and freedom from locusts, earthquake, and other natural disasters.

It is doubtful that contemporary witches were surprised or unduly distressed by this new policy. They would have expected any god worth his candle to offer material consideration in return for homage. And quite probably they had their own ideas about their new competitor's effectiveness in the witch business.

They underestimated, in fact they could not even conceive of, their new competitor's determination to corner the market as intermediary to the supernatural world.

The sorceresses from Thessaly and others of their ilk had necessitated laws against poisoning and enchantment, but not against the more ordinary functioning of the craft. In the fourth century the Christian emperors, Valentinian and Valens, changed this approach with a surge of persecution that was a precursor of terrors to come. No man was too influential, too learned, too wealthy, too popular to be attacked. The victims and their wives were tortured, their estates seized, their families broken up on the charges of sorcery and treason.

After the fall of the Roman empire, for hundreds of years the coexistence or enmity of witchcraft and Christianity was a matter of local option. No political force was strong enough to compel a consensus one way or the other in a territory of any size. However, as the church's power and organization grew, and her encroachment into the domain of witchcraft became more pervasive, her attitude toward witchcraft hardened into outright hostility. And she showed an increasing preoccupation with the devil and his adjuncts.

The Satan or satans of the Old and New Testaments were, in the originals, by no means the Prince of Darkness who emerged after centuries of priestly reworking and amendment of the original material. The notion of a fallen angel who had committed himself to a career of evil and who caused humans to do his work by taking possession of their minds and bodies developed during the Roman period, when Christianity was exposed to Babylonian, Syrian, and Alexandrian beliefs in demonology. As a control device the concept was excellent, and unconsciously church officers intensified, detailed, and burnished their stories of hellfire, the Arch Rebel, and his demonic legions.

In 872 A.D. a directive was issued which falsely purported to be the work of the fourth-century Council of Ankara, advising bishops and priests to weed out from among their flock the "pernicious practice of divination and magic, which was invented by the devil."

That first sounding of the trumpet was little affected by the directive's internal inconsistency in attempting to ridicule the witches' claims to power: "Nor is it to be overlooked that certain depraved women who have turned back after Satan and been seduced by the illusions and fantasies of demons believe and profess that they ride on various beasts during the night hours along with Diana, goddess of the pagans, and a countless multitude of women, and pass across many areas of the earth in the dead of the unwholesome night; and that they obey her commands as those of a mistress, and on certain nights are summoned to her service . . . though the unfaithful woman experiences all this only in the spirit she believes that it happens not in the mind but in the flesh."

In the meantime, the church continued to expand its activities in the area of materialistic gains for her parishioners achieved under the auspices of rite and chant and amulet. The transition to witchcraft was smooth. No doubt it was facilitated by the fact that many priests and nuns had been witches or the offspring of witches before entering the church and, consciously or unconsciously, transfused the disciplines of their first faith into the framework of their second.

Before the church was done, religious charms could be purchased to deal with every contingency from lost trinkets to successful bargaining at the fair, and a saint governed each aspect of secular life. St. Apollinaris cured the cripples. St. Luke was patron of the arts. St. Valentine brought lovers together. St. Vitus stilled a maddened brain and quieted the dancing mania. St.

Peter brought fishermen good luck. St. Hubert rescued dogs afflicted with rabies. And St. Fiacre shrunk hemorrhoids.

At this point the church could expunge the witches without robbing the people of vital services. The mood of the populace from lord to serf was propitious. The confusion and fear of hostile sorcery noted in the last chapter had peaked, and border warfare had burst upon the villages without warning, or the threat of it hung over their rooftops like smoke. The air was thick with social change, disease, and death. Fear and hatred crawled along people's nerves, waiting to be discharged.

The church struck. From every pulpit, and in the religious plays and pageants that were among the people's few enjoyments, warnings were sounded against those servants of the devil, the witches. They practiced enchantments to ensnare men's souls. They bewitched their bodies to their harm. They cavorted in obscene rites. They snatched babies from their cradles and ate their flesh to obtain evil powers. They kidnapped sweethearts and brought them to the devil to be ravished. The plague rode upon the breath of their curses. They poisoned men's food and drink. Their conjurings crippled the limbs. They used the lust of their bodies to lure men to hell. But their true pleasure came when they turned their bodies over to the beastly attentions of their familiars.

Panic which had been dispersed in all directions suddenly focused and hardened into murderous rage. Unfortunately, there was just enough truth in the church's accusations to make the witches' defense of themselves difficult. Worse, the witches were not organized into a single body and had no means of directing a unified counter-assault. First, witches were attacked with increasing impunity. Then local ordinances against witchcraft began to appear. By the tenth century, the church was the only legitimate dispensor of the supernatural in western Europe and had won virtual control of the field.

But the process was as uncertain as human emotion. Time and again in the centuries to come, growing corruption within the church drove people back to the witches. As the church became more interested in exercising power in her own right than in making secure the claims of others, the secular royalty that had been responsible for her suzerainty became dissatisfied with her services and jealous of her powers. Their subjects shared the disillusionment. The cost of the church's good offices had increased far in excess of general inflation. Worst of all, the corrupt lives of the clergy, from parish priest to Pope, created widespread unease as to their true ability either to work magic or save souls.

The attacks on the church began that would eventually culminate in the Protestant Reformation of the sixteenth century. Concomitantly, there was a movement to reform the church from within, led by such ascetics as St. Francis of Assisi. However, the common reaction from the masses of people on every level of the social scale was to return to the ancient practice of witchcraft.

To the church, all these responses formed a single threat. She reacted by tightening the screws of fear. In 1233, the Pope commissioned some Dominican monks to investigate one of the reform movements. The movement became known as the Albigensian heresy; the investigation bloomed into the Inquisition. Soon the church hit on the tactic of numbering the witches with the heretics, and the holocaust blazed.

The church had at her command all the power of the secular governments she controlled. The heretics the church found guilty were executed by the civil governments, often called the church's secular arm. She also had the power of entrenched organization and established lines of communication. In Europe, her spies were literally everywhere. She had the machinery of propaganda. Further, she was learning to apply the old trick of the Roman emperors: give the people a spectacle of blood which discharges emotion and inspires fear at the same time, while channeling both toward the intended victim.

Both the church and witchcraft altered drastically during the struggle. In the church, good men sickened of their task and bad men became unspeakable. The witch hunt sowed the seeds of clerical revolt; Martin Luther had been one such priest.

Witchcraft suffered more drastically.

CHAPTER THREE

Sadism

Persecution drove the witches underground. Just as the church had gone in for witchcraft, the witches, who went to mass in order to camouflage their true identities, became Christianized. Occasionally, the conversion was genuine. More often, such attendance resulted in the passive inclusion of some church language and forms in their own ritual.

For a growing number of witches, enforced Christianity crystalized into a fetish of perverse opposition. It was silly. It was ugly. But the hatred was real. It was during this time that the Black Mass developed its counterclockwise rituals and repugnant embellishments. There was never a charge made by some rabble-rousing priest with an overdeveloped imagination that some witch, seething with pent-up fury, did not try to substantiate.

They communed with evil spirits. They summoned devils. They ate babies, poisoned wells, raped men and women. They called forth plagues and unseasonable weather. They devised orgies of a nature to exhaust human strength and invention. They selected leaders to represent the Devil and worshipped his flesh in an imaginative variety of ways. They practiced homosexuality, bisexuality, bestiality, and, if one counts the pile-driving action of the oversized wooden phallus in the hand of the devil-priest, materiality as well. They developed and indulged obsessions about urine and feces and other generally unsavory objects such as corpses, rat's eyes, bat wings, and toad skin. These things were collected, cooked, consumed, bathed in, and smeared on. They devised and signed contracts full of elaborate clauses, selling their souls to Satan. In blood. There was a great deal of letting and spilling and splashing of blood. Blood and sex and nastiness grew into a cult of sadism.

Like fungus, sadism spread through the cults, replacing their original goals. Drugs heightened the macabre frenzy of their celebrations. Hallucinogenics and other drugs affecting nervous tissue had been a valued tool in the craft since the first magician made the first lucky discovery, but they had been used judiciously and with deference to the power inherent in them. In the sadism cults, the drug scene went wild. Malicious persons sponsored the revelry for their own amusement, or in order to have a terrorist group that would stop at nothing. Slowly, excesses leached the magic out of the sadism cults. Sorcery requires great discipline: patience, physical strength, and a concentrated mind. It is not congruent with psychosis, either inherent or drug-induced.

Not all the witches went this route. Some kept their craft sacred and secret, even from their families. Some fought back like soldiers and organized like soldiers; there will be more on this movement later.

The spread of sadism and psychosis among the

witches is not surprising. The times were fantastically cruel and mad. People could not safely walk the streets or country roads, day or night. The age indulged in torture, self-torture, incredible asceticism, sensory indulgence to what would seem to be the point of discomfort, celibacy in and out of monastic life, lusty sex, twisted sex, orgies of sex in and out of monastic life, reform and counter-reform, homicide, irresponsible rivalry among secular and religious leaders, intrigue on all levels, epidemics, the dancing mania, the hysterical attacks on the holy land first by adults, then by children. It was a nightmare period.

Of course, we have been talking about churches and movements and historical divisions. Individuals persist in being their own unique selves.

There were clerics who kept their witchcraft and their priesthood separate. Men and women met and made children and giggled in the night. Bishops governed whose primary concern was for the souls in their diocese and who privately recognized and respected the practitioners of an ancillary discipline. Lords maintained a respect for human dignity within the boundaries of their domains. Witches who were pious Christians kissed the cross and made their responses to the priest's litany in the approved manner, while going over in their minds the necessary steps for a potion they were about to brew. Christians died martyred at the hands of witch terrorists. Witches died martyred at the hands of Christians. Innocents, caught in the middle of a power struggle they neither desired nor understood, were martyred by both sides.

The Christians were in the majority; they had control of the government on the highest levels. The witches were martyred in vast numbers, in a holocaust of burning and torture.

From the church's point of view, it was a necessity. Reaction to the corruption within the clergy, the monasteries, and the convents, and to the travesty of two Popes battling with their armies and scheming with secular rulers to control the throne of St. Peter, had become so bitter that the church could not afford to allow the existence of an alternative for the people. Reaction was so violent that if the church had not already possessed the instruments of power, it seems likely that witchcraft would have triumphed, or at least have survived as a vital part of European life.

But the church had the power, and she had the numbers. Her courts tried the witches. The civil authorities to whom she handed them over for execution were church-educated, church-supported, as afraid as any of being accused of practicing witchcraft themselves. And, as has been pointed out, her spies crawled through the social structure like lice. Her orators whipped up tension and sent it spewing forth in the form of a mob, lusting for the blood of witches. Whether through civil or ecclesiastical trial or by the hands of the mob, the end for the witches was death.

Those who died at the hands of the mob had the easiest passing. The mobs beat and stoned their victims, putting out an eye here and tearing off an arm there, but they were rough and overeager and their victims soon died. The courts were experts in slow torture.

The currently approved historic line is that the martyred were harmless, if rattled, little old Christian ladies. Some of them were just that. But most of them were guilty as charged; they practiced magic. They divined the future. They worshipped other gods than Christ, or they worshipped Christ in a manner that caused the dignitaries in the Vatican to tear their robes.

Some of the witches were guilty of no more than doing their own thing: worshipping their own gods, performing their own rituals. Others were guilty of seditious action to win the right to be witches openly. Adherents of the Black Mass cults, and there were many of them, had usually done everything ascribed to them and probably a little more.

No degree of guilt can justify the methods that were used against them.

From the thirteenth century on, it was a matter of the greatest simplicity to have a person arrested for practicing witchcraft. All that was required was to arouse the neighbors' suspicion, hatred, or in some cases greed. Once arrested, the accused, regardless of social position, slid down the greased runways to his doom.

The most powerful victim of this madness was an entire order of knighthood, the Order of the Knights Templar, an organization that crossed national as well as feudal boundaries and possessed the wealth and prestige of a principality. It took a king to accuse them; and it took a vast financial embarrassment to motivate the king.

In 1307 Philip IV of France declared that the Knights Templar sold their souls to the Devil in festivals of horror during which babies were slaughtered and eaten. The order was officially nullified. Its estates were confiscated, and hundreds of its fifteen hundred members were executed. Fifty-four Templars were roped together and slowly cooked to death in a spectacular bonfire. Jacques de Moley, the order's Grand Master, was tortured unspeakably before he sank into the mercy of death.

Where the powerful cannot save themselves, the weak have no chance. Arrests were made on the strength of unpopularity. Nuns and priests tricked children into betraying their parents on the grounds that they were saving their souls from everlasting torment. Husbands and wives, siblings, relatives, former friends, business associates, masters and tenants, ladies and ladies-in-waiting, ex-sweethearts testified against each other.

It was a marvelously efficient means of terminating a relationship or settling a quarrel, as Katharina Kepler discovered almost too late.

Katharina was the mother of the famous Johannes Kepler, who at that time was Imperial Mathematician to the Hapsburg Emperor Rudolph III of Bohemia. There was little question that she was a witch. She foisted her herbs and potions on her fellow townsmen with the enthusiasm of a used car salesman. There was no question that she had been asking for it for some time. It required all of her son's genius to prevent her from getting it.

Interior evidence from a book that Johannes wrote for his own amusement suggests he shared his mother's enthusiasm for witchcraft. The book, *Somnium*, meaning "the dream," was a thinly disguised autobiography written in a popular literary form of the day. The story shows the character that represents Katharina employing her craft to conjure up spirits to advise her son on a voyage to the moon. Subsequently, through the help of the spirits, the son reaches the moon without requiring the use of a vehicle. When Johannes finished the book, he sent the manuscript home to his mother's town. Unknown to him, it was passed around to some of the more literate townspeople.

Katharina gossiped almost as vigorously as she hustled herbs. When a crony of hers, Ursala, became adulterously pregnant and obtained an abortion, Katharina could not resist telling her younger son. He was as good as a broadcast station.

Out of considerable pique and the necessity of salvaging her reputation, Ursala denied her pregnancy and abortion, claiming the true story was that her week's illness had been brought on by one of Katharina's curses. Ursala's brother, who was the barber—in those days that meant also demi-surgeon—of Duke Johann Friedrich of Wurtemberg, obviously a man of considerable influence, believed his sister. He had read Johannes' book.

He, along with Ursala, her cuckolded husband, and the town judge (who had been jilted by one of Katharina's daughters) were nursing their mutual grievances in the town pub over a bottle, or perhaps several, when Katharina happened by. The barber drunkenly pulled his sword, jabbing it at Katharina's neck, and mumbled that she had better remove the curse from his sister if she knew what was good for her.

It was Katharina's particular personality quirk that she never knew what was good for her. Obviously she should have drawn in her witch's horns, but she was a bully and accustomed to having her own way in that town.

The next day she sued Ursala for slander.

The barber compiled a case against her as long as a football field, including such compelling arguments as the fact that she had been reared by a known witch who was later executed as a witch, and his accusations were corroborated by a flock of eager witnesses.

The town's long-dormant hostility towards Katharina was already coming to a head when she lost her temper at a poor girl who bumped into her with a heavy load of bricks on the way to the kiln. Katharina cursed her on the spot. The girl suffered a temporary paralysis of the arm.

The time had passed when Katharina could get away with that kind of malice. The girl ran screaming to the town authorities. Katharina, finally perceiving the seriousness of her position, applied her usual bad judgment and offered the magistrate a rather cheap silver chalice to drop the court case against her.

The wonder is she was not lynched.

Before she was done with her temper and her bungling, she had been imprisoned, chained, and tortured. In France, Spain, Portugal, Italy, and parts of Germany, she would have died that way. But in Katharina's country respect for witches went deep; after fourteen months of imprisonment and fourteen months of carefully executed legal maneuvering by Johannes, Katharina was released into his care on the condition that she never again return to Leonberg.

In the usual case, whether the bad temper was on the side of the witch or her accuser, all that was needed for arrest was an accusation. At the trial, hearsay was counted as sufficient evidence. After all, such evidence was later tested. The judges, in the name of justice, insisted on confirmation—unless, of course, the witch confessed. Testing persons accused of sorcery became a profession in itself. Witch finders traveled from village to village, plying their trade, exchanging their services for fees: so much for an examination; double that amount for conviction.

The scale of payment encouraged irregularities. The witch finders' tests insured them and, centuries later in the inevitable reaction to the atrocities, became one reason for the belief that all the accused were innocent.

The preliminary professional test went by the name

of *watching*, a word that describes it as nicely as *fish* describes shark. The accused was stripped, often before the entire town—this in a period in which people often wore a covering garment when they washed. After all hair had been hacked off with razors that had made the growing of beards more a necessity than a choice, the skin was examined minutely for traces of witch's marks. Then the accused was bound by cords that dug through the soft flesh until they rested firmly on bone and kept awake and starved for at least twenty-four hours.

If the witch finder was skillful with the ropes, the accused often broke down and confessed before the watching was at an end. If she was recalcitrant, contemporary jurisprudence allowed the witch finder to declare any creature the size of a mosquito or larger that settled on her person to be her familiar come to suck. Positive evidence of this nature required that the testing continue.

Pricking required a bit more finesse than watching. The test centered around a talent some sorceresses had claimed for themselves: the ability to control the flow of blood. It hardly seemed likely that they would care to exercise this talent during the testing, so the witch finders were forced to become skillful at selecting a thick callus or an old scar and thrusting the needle in slantwise. Perfectionists in this business disdained half-way measures and carried on their persons collapsible needles.

The king of prickers was Witchfinder General (the title was his own composition) Mathew Hopkins. He charged the villages twenty shillings a visit and rarely rode away without the double fee of forty. Greed eventually made him careless; he was caught manufacturing evidence and hung, but not before he could boast of being responsible for the deaths of over two hundred persons.

It was said that a witch would float where an honest man sank. This saying was the origin of the custom of dunking, so effective in obtaining confessions that its use spread to crime detection in other areas. A variety of machinery submerged the accused under water for a minute, a minute and a half, two minutes—whatever was judged to be just short of death. If the accused witch died during the testing, her family had the comfort of knowing that in dying she had proven her innocence. Those that sank and were pulled out still alive and unconfessed were likely to find themselves back under water while the witch finder checked out his procedure against the possibility of error. If the suspect floated, it was considered evidence strong enough to convict her.

She was not, however, killed on the spot. Even after she had been declared a witch, her judges strove for a confession that would remove any doubt that justice had miscarried, and would pave the way for her contrition and eventual salvation. Confessions were elicited by torture. It was not necessary to develop a profession for coping with this aspect of the business. Europe already had torturers aplenty.

Flogging was basic. Although crude, it was remarkably effective, whether accomplished with the long braided-leather whip or with the shorter, metal-tipped cat-o'-nine-tails. A good flogging consisted of about thirty blows; a hundred could cripple a man for life. Tack on fifty more and he might die. Four or five good floggings usually stripped a decade off a man's life.

Special pincers were designed to rip fingernails from their pads. Generally, this was done after needles had been pushed under them or through their quicks.

Thumb screws, a variety of clamp, were tightened until the skin burst and the victim's blood and muscle squirted out the sides of the ruined finger. The same principle was applied to the foot with the use of a collapsible metal boot that could and did turn the foot to a cupful of red pulp.

Racks were essentially sets of pullies rigged to pull in opposite directions and tied to wrists and ankles, stretching the body until muscle, ligament, and tendon tore and joints dislocated.

Hot irons were used deftly to sear skin, destroy the muscle beneath, or remove an eye.

These systems of pain were applied singly or in succession—whatever stubborn silence made necessary or the judge's whim suggested.

Prolonged torture has a way of intruding itself upon the mind so that even years of discipline and a natural proclivity for psychic control are rendered useless. The witches confessed along with the non-witches.

Many, both witches and non-witches, recanted as soon as the pain stopped shorting out the nerve tracks in the brain. They were again persuaded, with renewed vigor.

The aftermath of the confession was death by flame or by the rope. Usually the victims welcomed it.

The records of those who were forced into the initial steps of the procedure but escaped the final phases are incomplete. Such escapes were rare. Even the judges were weighted down by the numbers of the condemned. One of them wrote: "The seats destined for criminals in our courts of justice are blackened with persons accused of this guilt [witchcraft]. There are not judges enough to try them. Our dungeons are gorged with them. No day passes that we do not render our tribunals bloody by the dooms which we pronounce, or in which we do not return to our homes discountenanced and terrified at the horrible confessions which we have heard. And the Devil is accounted so good a master, that we cannot commit so great a number of his slaves to the flames but what there shall arise from their ashes a sufficient number to supply their place."

Something like nine million persons were killed as witches.

The last siege was the worst. The Protestant Reformation was spawned in the soil of ecclesiastic corruption and the savagery of the Inquisition. The old church struck out in every direction with increased violence and less reason; and the new church was as frenzied as the old. The Protestants were attempting to return to the original concept of Christianity as a religion whose emphasis was on salvation. They had no intention of aligning themselves with the witches against the mother church. The witchcraft of both was detestable to them. Luther phrased it succinctly: "I would have no compassion on the witches. I would burn them all."

The new churches did their best.

And the rationalists and materialists who followed them—those who question even the evidence of their senses and will admit the existence of nothing they cannot pinch—were equally destructive to the beliefs which were the essence of the craft, although they spared the bodies of the witches themselves. Witches born were channeled into other professions. Witches who, despite the new environment of skepticism and scorn, managed to complete their training were likely to find themselves with precious few adherents and a steadily shrinking field of usefulness.

Today, the Western world has put the latest creations of science in the place once held by sorcery. The atom bomb, nerve gas, biological warfare, and the family of pollutants have led us to suspect that scientists, too, can be malevolent. The nature worship of witchcraft might be safer for mankind than the destruction of nature achieved by the rationalists and materialists.

CHAPTER FOUR

Covens and Sabbats

Historian William Lecky, a lifelong skeptic on the subject of the supernatural, confessed wryly, "If we considered witchcraft probable, a hundredth part of the evidence we possess would have placed it beyond the region of doubt. If it were a natural but improbable fact, our reluctance to believe it would have been completely stifled by the multiplicity of the proofs."

This admission is interesting for a number of reasons, the chief one being that the larger part of the "multiplicity of proofs" consists of those "voluntary" confessions described in the last chapter.

One of the ubiquitous tenets of witchcraft, regardless of time and place, is that exposure of craft secrets to the uninitiated eats away the strength of magic as oxygen rusts iron. The medieval witches kept no written records, nor did they speak except to chosen novitiates bound to secrecy or in order to put an end to torture. Similarly, the African Dingaka Association, a forward-looking, contemporary society of four thousand witches, has repeatedly been forced to refuse to cooperate with delegations from the medical profession who want to study their methods.

Since witches are mum except under the duress of pain, how can we be sure that any of the confessions were valid?

First of all, even the spurious confessions, the ones that the whips and the racks ripped out of innocent persons, compose a surprisingly accurate and consistent picture of the witches of the time. The same is the case with the lying testimony for the prosecution delivered by malicious witnesses.

The salient point is that the accused and the witnesses against them knew what to say. They knew what a witch was, what a witch did. Today, if an average layman were tortured to force him to confess that he was a doctor, although he had never set foot in medical school, he could put together a convincing story. After all, he has seen doctors, he has been a patient, he has friends who have been patients. Medicine is a profession that interests people. It is talked about, joked about, grumbled about, written up in plays. Even a child could give a recognizable word-picture of a doctor.

Before the church began the holocaust, witches conducted their business openly. Everyone joined in the celebration of their sabbats. One of the functions of the sabbats was to draw the entire community into a cohesive whole. No wonder men and women who had never muttered a charm or gone through the motions of the simplest ritual could manufacture a story that would satisfy the townspeople.

This theory is confirmed by the fact that the confessions were remarkably alike from village to village, province to province, and country to country. The significant differences came with time. Further, confessions made without torture contain the same information as forced confessions. In theory, torture was never permitted in English courts; and in fact it rarely was used. The English witches who confessed voluntarily have been passed off by the cynics as attention-freaks, people who would rather be roasted than ignored. No doubt there were some who died that way, but all of them?

In any case, the confessions were remarkably similar throughout Europe, including England. But the passing of time brought significant changes. The contrast between a thirteenth-century and an eighteenth-century witch is like that between a sunny meadow and a swamp in the dark of night. By the eighteenth century, satanism with all its foolishness and sadism had swept through the craft like a plague.

The pre-Christian and un-Christian sabbats were agricultural celebrations designed to honor and to stimulate nature. The specific goal varied with the season. The leader might be a witch-priest, a priest-witch, or several of both. Peasant worshippers attended as best they could, depending on how far away the festival was and how lenient their masters were about such things. The early Middle Ages was a jumbled period, with beliefs from far-off places in strange gods and goddesses influencing once stable communities. Two neighboring counties might have widely differing practices, depending on the beliefs of their local lords and the special talents of their witches. The process was one of assimilation rather than conflict; often the same people attended without guilt or blame several different sabbats.

Whatever the particulars of the occasion, there would be rituals designed to help the farmer with his fields and to extend human welfare. Ceremonies would honor certain spirits or gods. Sacrifices would be offered at certain sabbats, and some of those sacrifices would be human. More often than not, it was a case of a man willingly giving up his life for the common good. One life to stave off plague; one life to stave off defeat. It was a hard bargain, people felt, but a fair one. Among the Druids and various other cults, after the sacrifice had been offered, the corpse would be sliced up and ritually eaten, not as a feast of evil but as a communion with the spirit the body had contained. And unquestionably many of the fertility rites involved sexual intercourse, which often took place in the very fields they were hoping to fructify.

After the rituals that required concentration and precision had been completed, there would be feasting, accompanied by drinking or drug taking (or both), music, dancing, singing, marching, and delighted shouting. The celebrants would be gaily robed, or perhaps naked and adorned with body paint. The witches and priests would have on their masks and headdresses and all the insignia of their power. There would be joy and mystery and power, and a deep sense of wellbeing; for what was necessary had been done. Nature had been honored. The rhythms of life had been enhanced.

If the church had embraced the witches, before long in some of the provinces the people would have flocked to the seasonal sabbats in Christ's name. Without doubt, sabbats were held secretly in his name. If they were discovered by the church, the sabbat ended in terror, trial, and torture.

Persecution's most immediate effect was to change the character of the sabbat. In those districts, and they were by far the most numerous, where the church could enforce its injunction, the sabbats abruptly ceased to be public. Certain festivals and parts of others had always been nocturnal, but illegality made darkness the rule. Even at night, with the threat of exposure hovering over them, the joy and spontaneity of the celebrants dried up. There remained only the necessity of performing the ceremonies that would being large crops and healthy babies and create harmony between man and nature.

But as fear and hatred set the community against the witches, this purpose too died. When their communities' welfare ceased to be the concern of the witches, their eyes turned inward. Their attention centered on the coven. Originally, the coven was the pagan version of parish, comprising the witch and the community, the witch and those he led in ritual. However, as witchcraft was forced underground, safety dictated that only practicing witches be allowed in the covens. Increased vigilance on the part of their oppressors further reduced the membership of individual covens; and satanism eventually set the number of members at thirteen, mocking the thirteen who sat at the Last Supper.

To those engaged in the theater of the profane, the thirteen count became inviolate: twelve female witches and one devil-priest. Each decade had its favorite costumes for the two roles. And each successive decade elaborated these parts. The sabbat was transformed into an orgy of sadism. Drugs to still the witches' very realistic fear of arrest were taken in increasing amounts and new combinations. They had a surprising variety to choose from. Belladonna jam, consumed sparingly, produced an incredible high followed by amnesia. Aconite speeded up the heartbeat and made the witch feel giddy. The crusaders had discovered hashish and laudanum, the tincture of opium, and merchants learned it was profitable to keep them supplied with these drugs after they returned home. This was the period in which the Irish invention of *usequebaugh* was transfixing alchemists, most of whom were witches, and their happy friends under the international latin name of *aqua vitae*, "water of life"—that is, distilled alcohol. The lilies of the valley often grew on Jimson weed, a drug that will be discussed more thoroughly later on. A wild fungus introduced to growing wheat, harvested, winnowed, ground, and baked, produced a bread rich in raw ergot, the first stage of LSD, and had its consumers running pell-mell through the streets shouting, "Halloo!" In 1532, Francisco Pizarro simultaneously discovered Peru and the harmless-looking coca leaves that the subjects of the Great Inca kept cramming into their mouths. By the seventeenth century, this crude form of cocaine was a familiar drug in Europe.

With their anxieties and reservations dispelled, excitement heightened, and reality itself shot through with explosive colors and dancing images, the covens would spit in the church's prudish eye with orgiastic sexual debauches in which the inventiveness and stamina of their members were tested to the utmost. These were the covens that enjoyed the drama of making an altar out of a nude woman's body, incense out of feces, and holy water out of urine. These were the covens that loved the horror of dumping corpses out of their graves, the thrill of random murder, cooking up babies' fingers, drinking out of skulls, whipping friend and foe until the skin cracked, gorging themselves on red bread —human flesh—and generally wallowing in blood and pain.

Although most of the satanists were not witches at all in the real sense of the word, there were those among them who still possessed compelling talents which they used to attract followers and to provide their own amusement. But they were not about to share the source of their primacy with anyone, and more often than not the rites they performed before the coven were false or adulterated, the real work having been accomplished before the meeting.

Cursing methods proliferated in form and variety during the Middle Ages, as did all kinds of divination. Looking into the future, diagnosing character, finding precious metals lying under the soil, and detecting the presence of spirits were popular among the sorcerers, as were magical travel, summoning up various spirits (or perhaps rendering them temporarily visible to non-witches by the use of drugs), and brewing potions for as many needs, including invisibility, as the church had attempted to meet with its amulets and saints.

The rest of the group, at their best, were rebellious youngsters. Drunk and reckless with too much and too frequent drug-taking, they would invade the church services or festivals, instituted to replace the sabbats, with laughter and coarse jokes and their own quick, gay, catchy, obscene "devil's tunes," often dressed in clothing suggestive of their association. It was a prank that often led to the thinning of their ranks.

At their worst they are best forgotten.

When a coven existed as a disciplined terrorist group, function was more important than numbers or costume. Such groups were kept small so that capture and confession under torture would expose as few as possible. All the power residing within a coven was aimed at the representatives of the establishment. Cursing, including casting the evil eye, was the witches' hand weapon, so to speak—always at the ready, always frightening, and surprisingly often effective. Execution by effigy had a marvelous propaganda effect in addition to its specific goal. In England, open hostilities between the Christians and the witches were touched off when a Saxon witch accepted a commission to kill the Norman king by the device of sticking lead pins into his waxen image. To prove his fitness for the job, the witch first applied his talents to a commoner, Richard de Sowe. The witch was not one to rush his work. Three days after he had pierced de Sowe's effigy with the first pin, he thrust the last one into the region of the heart. De Sowe died, and so frightened one of the conspirators that he confessed the plot to the authorities.

The witches practiced their own style of germ warfare, inflicting on their enemies diseases painful or fatal depending on their goal. They hexed entire herds of cattle, poisoned wells, and called down rain to ruin the harvest and winds to dry up the sprouting seeds. Church supporters were threatened, kidnapped, beaten, crippled, and robbed. Torture was met with torture. Execution with execution. Sometimes, for a time, the guerrilla forces prevailed. An entire district would return to the ancient practices. Then the better organized and better equipped church-supported groups would move in again. This large-scale fighting is usually disguised in history books as feuding between rival lords, as indeed it was. What the books fail to mention is that the rivalry was over not only territory but also the right to worship.

Medieval witches were not addle-pated old ladies. Neither were they the impressive, attractive leaders they had once been. Even the serious-minded terrorists had been influenced by the smoke and flickering lights and savagery of the Black Mass. The profile of the witch was changing.

As a matter of fact, the sex had already changed.

Although the pre-Christian witch was sometimes female, more often than not the role was a male one. In the Middle Ages there were still male witches, but they were generally executed under another name: sorcerer, warlock, heretic. To the courts, *witch* had come to imply female.

It was only very late in the history of organized European witchcraft, however, that witches came to be thought of as old and ugly. Earlier, it was taken for granted that any witch worth a bag of salt had mastered her own body. In some, the capacity was said to go as far as the ability to change from human to animal form. Even in the least skillful, it involved the ability to slow down the aging process and maintain a pleasing aspect. Witches of both sexes were notorious for using the beauty of their bodies to confound Christians.

Before it became too dangerous, witches had borne on their bodies the mark of their calling. Its nature varied according to custom. Most often it was a deliberate scarification made at the time of initiation into the cult. The flesh was incised and ashes were rubbed into the wounds to make them heal in raised scars. Among the theater of the profane, it was fashionable to make a wound that resembled a stylized devil's claw.

The witch finders claimed they had another distinguishing mark, a special teat for nourishing their familiars. The witches did, in fact, have familiars, or spirits housed in animal shapes; and they nourished them; but not with witch's teats. Such familiars were more often found in large towns and cities than in the countryside. The witches' magic was based on agriculture, not on buildings and trade, so they brought something filled with the spirit of nature into the smoky towns with them. When they screamed out in their confessions that they fed these familiars with substance from their own bodies, they were referring to the blood they sacrificed as spiritual nourishment by nicking their fingers and shaking the drops of blood onto the creatures' food. The spirit within the flesh of the cat or dog or goat or hare or squirrel or cricket or toad accepted the blood as a love offering while the beast ate the food.

It was also charged that the witches lay nightly with their familiars in demonic rites of lust. Of the satanists it was probably true. The satanists were literal-minded and more attentive to detail than to comfort. For the mystics it was probably also true, in a different sense.

The familiar spirits were not the only inhabitants of the spirit world who lay with witches. The practice which was occasional among the pre-Christians became more and more common among the satanists. They thought it chic to have a spirit lover. The terminology developed to keep pace with the custom. Incubi, the witches' lovers, were first referred to as spirits, then as evil spirits, then as demons or imps of hell. In going over the confessions it is difficult to determine whether the intercourse mentioned occurred with an actual spirit or with the head of the coven acting for a spirit.

Succubi, the female demons, were if anything more ardent than incubi. Not content with exercising their lusts on warlocks, they pursued wholesome young Christian men, trying to capture their souls in the net of their compelling charms. One young Christian, chased through the streets by a lustful female demon, ran home, slamming his door shut in her face. With a low laugh, she walked through the solid door and began enticing him shamelessly. The young man ran screaming to his bishop for help. That dignitary may have been a little put out that no gorgeous succubi was bearding him in his lair. At any rate, he informed the young man coldly that to be attractive to the demons of hell was suspicious in itself. He recommended fasting and prayer, and regretted that he would not be able to permit the young man to take communion until he should rid himself of his demon suitor. It is quite possible that some of the succubi were in fact young women of the satanist covens who were amusing themselves by scaring the tights off the Christians.

In pre-Christian times, initiation usually implied that a young person was being ceremoniously introduced into the adult community. Witches became witches through a lengthy apprenticeship which involved living at a witch's side and doing his chores over a number of years while slowly acquiring the necessary disciplines. But when witchcraft became illegal, the decision to join a coven became a crucial turning point in an individual's life. With Church spies everywhere, it was an equally critical moment for the coven.

The satanists were inclined to go in drag, with the head of the cult wearing his devil suit or animal spirit costume when he first officially contacted the prospective member. There would be lengthy haggling about the sale of her soul, followed by the usual contract.

Satanist or terrorist, the initiation ceremony was performed with all the pomp the coven could muster. The terrorists had a desperate need to impress the novice with the seriousness of her step and the agonizing consequences if she should betray their trust. For both groups the occasion was a victory celebration: one more for their side, and one less for the Christians.

During the ceremony, Christianity was officially renounced. Some of the covens recruited young, the witches leading their toddling children up to the altar to lisp their devotion to the Devil; some were carried in arms and the declarations made for them. Too many betrayals by too many children soon put an end to this custom.

In the terrorist covens, as many of the old rites as could be remembered and executed were put into practice at this time. The coven's leader, wearing robes and a headdress that were patched heirlooms, would sacrifice an animal, lead the coven in offering it to the spirit-gods, and commend the new member to their care.

Naturally, in the theater of the profane, the initiation was celebrated by a Black Mass in which the sacrifice and the communion bread were human. In both groups, varying amounts of food, drugs, and alcohol were a part of the ritual.

All of this is something of an oversimplification, of course. Some individuals and some covens obligingly confined themselves to the two patterns we have been discussing, but more often than not the individuals and the covens existed in the customary human muddle in which pure types are an anomaly. Terrorists and satanists merged. And with typical human perversity they merged not only with each other, but now and again with Christian groups as well.

An illustrative case is that of Joan of Arc. Serious scholarship has uncovered strong evidence to suggest that she was a heretic or a witch or both. Throughout her trial she refused to name Christ specifically. Instead she spoke ambiguously of "my lord." During the entire time she was battling for her life, she would not recite the Paternoster aloud. She claimed her authority to lead troops in battle and to engage the foe at specified times came from St. Michael, who appeared to her in the flesh to give her her orders. However, although questioned repeatedly on this point, she never did state whether at the time of his appearances St. Michael's flesh was naked.

It is certain that adherents of the old religion would have had no objection to following a witch of proven ability into battle. If, as seems likely, Joan was a witch, the common people who flocked to her standard and the flashing success of her campaigns take on an even deeper meaning than that of nascent nationalism. Joan's fight would have been essentially a crusade for the old religion. She was convinced, and convinced the men who fought her battles and the women who fed her armies, that once the English were driven from the land and the Dauphin seated on his rightful throne, he would allow his people to return to their ancient ways and throw off the foreign religion along with the foreign king.

Joan has been accused of being homosexual, a practice congruent with medieval sorcery. It is unlikely that the truth of the issue can be established now. The charge seems to be based on her preference for male clothing and her continuing pleas during the trial that she be allowed to have her women about her. This foundation is rather weak. Convenience alone would suggest the use of masculine clothing. Women's styles of the day were not designed for athletics, and playing down her female shape and personality would have been only discreet in a situation where she was in constant close association with large numbers of men. Furthermore, she was at an age for which dress-up would have had an appeal of its own, unrelated to sexual drives. Her begging for her women was surely a cry for protection, whatever her sexual nature. One hates to speculate over-long on what she must have gone through every night at the hands of her English soldier-jailors.

Her sexual inclinations would seem to be strictly her own affair, for she did not indulge them. There is no record of her having had an affair of any kind. She was a serious-minded girl, intent on her mission. Heretic or witch or Christian, her life was dominated by religion.

The same cannot be said of her right-hand man and military advisor, Giles de Rais, the Marshal of France. De Rais was a witch, the leader of a Dianist cult. He was also a practicing homosexual. The real-life model for the cleaned up children's story of *Bluebeard*, De Rais was found guilty of kidnapping, raping, and murdering an extraordinarily large number of young boys as a prerequisite to his rites of conjuration. His arrest occurred years after Joan's trial. No one knows the degree to which he indulged his hobbies before Joan's death.

Time is the enemy of any investigation of medieval witchcraft. We can guess, accumulate evidence to support our guesswork, and gradually develop a theory, but the specifics are lost in the confusion of the years. Even the outlines are not as firm as we would like.

Both the sorcerers and their enemies, however, were agreed as to the potency of witch power. It is we in the twentieth century who demur. Mind-reading, shape-changing, levitation, foretelling the future, summoning and conversing with the dead and with spirits fierce and gentle, mineral and water witching, healing and killing magic were as real as color television to them. Both Christian dogma and thousands of witches acknowledged the physical existence of hell and the corporeal presence of Satan, and many claimed to have arrived at their conclusions via personal experience. For these people, faery rings, water sprites, and impish mischief were not uncommon, and divine intervention was a daily occurrence. They saw the solar system and all the stars moving around this earth in time to the music of the spheres and never doubted that they themselves were the chief actors on the stage of creation and the principal concern of the creator.

Centuries later, only one or two of their convictions have been positively disproved. The climate of conviction, on the other hand, has reversed itself, so that in our minds a person who held one of these beliefs would be suspect in any of his opinions. Their times were different than ours. Their values were different. And the difference was great enough to make it impossible to know what testimony to ignore and what to weigh heavily.

It is interesting that two centuries of skepticism have not completely smothered the rumors that wild talents exist. Reports of these talents come from every culture and every race on earth, and from every time period—including our own. Our scientists are kept busy explaining them away. We cannot reverse the flow of time, but we can turn our attention to those witches who still practice their craft and employ their talents.

CHAPTER FIVE

Where Witches Live

The tragic aspect of the management of news is that so little really needs to be suppressed from above. If an idea can be so successfully discredited that no one will believe in it, no news connected with it will exist to be suppressed.

No organized conspiracy exists today to prevent true information about witches from reaching the ears of the public. None is needed. Once the maxim that only a superstitious dolt believed in magic had been set in motion, people's anxiety took over. As in the case of the emperor's clothes, those who see deny the evidence out of cowardice. Community leaders and educators are the most fervent in their blind denial of the possibility of magic.

The motives for this negation go deeper than hypocrisy. The anti-supernatural climate of opinion is so strong that most adults refuse to believe the evidence of their own senses. They, in turn, continue the process of brainwashing by insisting that this, that, and the other event cannot have occurred, are only superstitious nonsense, illusion, coincidence, or some other of the set of rationalizations current in our society.

In consequence, witchcraft cannot function among us in the only manner in which it can be a viable force: as a working, productive part of society. The magic that is practiced in this country is ghetto magic. Hostility has pushed sorcery to the back alleys of our cities and the back woods of our rural districts. Even there, it is practiced in secrecy that is half shame. Too many traditions have been lost. Too often the best candidates for witchhood have refused to live a ghetto life and have turned their talents to safer and more respected professions.

So while the vestigial magic that survives smog and asphalt and mass media is interesting, to investigate witches in the full strength of their craft we will have to turn our attention to those places where sorcery still thrives.

Africa is the first place that comes to mind and one of the great sources of modern witchcraft. Strong pulses of African sorcery have enriched Western witchcraft at different times and places throughout recorded history. African magic is so dynamic that it shows promise of surviving the onslaught of mechanized civilization and continuing to be a functioning part of contemporary African life. A book soon to be released in this series dealing with black witchcraft from ancient Egypt to modern-day African witches and their distant cousins in the black communities of this country would make a discussion of the subject here redundant.

Fortunately, other magic-oriented peoples exist who have the additional virtue of being more accessible to us in terms of travel time.

The Jívaro of South America are ideal for our purposes, because they are untouched by Western skepticism and in fact by almost any aspect of urban society. Even today, when both anthropologists and Christian missionaries thirst for new material, these tribes are rarely visited because of their tendency to prefer the heads of outsiders mounted on poles.

The Jívaro, whose villages dot the banks of the Ecuadorian Amazon, are headhunters. Today, when experts on the subject assure us that most human populations are rapidly breeding themselves out of any possible chance for a decent standard of living, they have a remarkably stable balance of births and deaths. Like the Plains Indians of the United States in the early 1800s and the feudal lords of medieval Europe, the Jívaro have their own preferred method of population control. It is a specialized form of war game in which increased territory is not the object of the hostilities. Enemy heads are taken as counters that provide enormous status to the killer and his tribe. *Enemy* in the Jívaro sense implies an opponent rather than an implacable foe who is intent on conquest and exploitation.

Witches flourish among the Jívaro. Probably few societies in the history of man have had as many witches per unit of population as they.

They do not claim as a people to have a superior aptitude for magic. Rather, they are grateful for having available to them a superior means of uncovering occult talent. *Natema*, a powerful hallucinogenic drug, perhaps more effective as a mind-bender than LSD, is the key to Jívaro sorcery. Their witches say that *natema* is the door to the real universe, and that the world the non-user experiences is a pitiable illusion.

Natema, the witches say, arouses the senses. Once its power has entered the human body, a man sees with his own eyes the world of the spirits that is invisible to him without the drug. The usual invisibility of the spirits does not reduce their impact on the world of man. Therefore, according to the Jívaro, it is only good sense to drink *natema* as the first step toward becoming an actor in the supernatural universe rather than an object being acted upon.

The significance of *natema* in the practice of sorcery is just beginning to be understood in the academic world. Those few Western explorers who had traveled up the Amazon into the dense reaches of jungle that serve as the Jívaro's home had dismissed their accounts of witchcraft and everything related to it as childish fantasies. Recently, however, one student, Michael J. Harner, had the curiosity and the courage to drink the potion the witches claimed was the only door to the spirit world and the only means of participating in magic.

After ingesting the beverage, Mr. Harner found himself in an environment stranger than the jungle. He was conversing with creatures whose bodies looked human but who had the heads of birds, and with others that were as big and frightful as dragons. These beings informed him that they were the true gods of this world. With their help, he flew through inner stellar space towards the outer limits of the galaxy.

The drug that powered Mr. Harner's trip and the magic of the Jívaros comes from the *Banistereopsis* vine and is found throughout Central and South America. To brew the potion, leaves are stripped from the vine and boiled in water, together with chunks from the vine's woody stalk. Chemically, the resultant tea has been found to contain harmaline, harmine, and traces of dimethyltryptamine (DMT). Called *yaje* in Colombia, *caapi* in Brazil, and *ayahuasa* in Peru, the drink produces vivid heightening of sound, taste, smell, and sight, in addition to the mystic visions that last from three to seven hours. Initially the drug is apt to upset the gastrointestinal tract, bringing on nausea, diarrhea, and even vomiting. However, repeated doses accustom the body to its use. Witches rarely suffer from these symptoms.

Among the Jívaro witches, as in effective sorcery anywhere, drug-taking is not random but functional. The witches drink *natema* because it opens the door to the spirit world and allows the witch to acquire his own pack of *tsentsak*. The *tsentsak* are legion, shaped like figures from a psychedelic dream: giant butterflies, brilliant serpents, elephant-sized jaguars, and forms unknown to the world of man. In behavior they are something between a virus and a guided rocket. By following certain procedures, a witch can obtain a force of *tsentsak* who will perch on his head and shoulders and cling to his arms, alert to do his bidding.

There are both healing witches and blighting witches in Jívaro sorcery. They are opposite numbers in a conflict on the supernatural level that is similar to the headhunting contests conducted by the tribe's warriors. Both kinds of witches go through identical training, and both use the *tsentsak* in their long duels for the life or death of the object of their conjurations.

It is important to realize that the blighting witch is not performing bootleg magic against one of his own. He will only attack victims outside his immediate community, and usually outside his tribe, so that the victim is nominally his enemy and the death will benefit his people in addition to being a professional victory for himself.

The witches are professionals. Payment is necessary to obtain their services.

After a witch has agreed to take on an assignment, his first act is to drink the *natema* that allows him to enter the real stage of battle and activates the *tsentsak*. In the first hour of darkness, the witch sneaks up to the house of his victim. As soon as he has positioned himself in a safe hiding place, he drinks green tobacco juice. The juice strengthens his psychic powers, enabling him to set loose the *tsentsak* on the enemy.

The wound at first is painless. The victim putters around his house unaware that an attack has been made. Inside his body, the *tsentsak* begin their work. "Multiply" is the wrong word for their action; "fester" is inexact. The presence of the *tsentsak* is inimical to health. The victim's strength is vitiated, and without help his condition will worsen.

Peculiarly enough, the absence of *tsentsak* in the victim's body can be more serious than their presence. If the blighting witch's *tsentsak* were strong enough to pass entirely through the victim's body, leaving only an empty wound, the attack is fatal. Nothing can be done for the injured man except to wait the days or weeks it takes him to die.

When prolonged sickness makes the victim suspect that he has been the object of malignant witchcraft, he goes to one of the healing witches in his village.

The healer cannot diagnose his patient's condition until he, too, has entered the spirit world. *Natema*, green tobacco juice, *piripiri* (another hallucinogenic), and evening shadows are the necessary conditions for an examination. When this combination is achieved, the healer's eyes can penetrate flesh and see what lies beneath. When the healer sees one of the blighting witch's *tsentsak* lying among the bowels of his patient, a duel in sorcery begins.

Usually, the healer recognizes the *tsentsak* and by

this means identifies his opposite number. The information is important only in terms of possible revenge. The cure can take place without it. This begins with the healer whistling, then singing, a curing song. The song excites his *tsentsak*, making them eager to begin their task. At the proper moment, he vomits two of them from their residence in his stomach up into the buccal cavity. These two will act as his personal watchdogs, protecting him from the blighting witch's weapons. Additional *tsentsak* hover like an aura or a band of protective angels around his person. While he works, the healer nourishes and strengthens them by taking frequent sips of the green tobacco juice. Thus armed and protected, the healer sucks the blighting witch's weapons out of his patient's body, drawing them into his own mouth.

Without the presence of his watchdogs, the enemy *tsentsak* would race down his gullet, flinging themselves into his stomach and sickening him with the same disease that had afflicted his patient. Instead, while they are trapped in his mouth, the healer's *tsentsak* cage the enemy weapons within the material objects in which they customarily dwell themselves.

After the blighting witch's *tsentsak* are safely imprisoned within the objects, the healer takes the objects out of his mouth and shows them to his patient, saying, "Here are the spirits that were making you sick."

The patient sees the objects and believes those are the spirits' own persons. The witches are aware of this misapprehension and even encourage it. It is pointless to try to paint a picture of the spirit world for the non-witch. Better to give him something he can see with his deluded eyes and take comfort in than to try to force on him a truth he could not comprehend. Furthermore, the misapprehension is not true deception, since the spirit actually lies within the objects shown the patient. (This relationship touches a problem rationalists have been disputing with witches since the seventeenth century. The rationalists will catch a witch performing sleight-of-hand or a stunt of ventriloquism and cry fraud. The witches vainly try to explain that the trick is merely packaging for the true sorcery hidden within.)

After the enemy weapons have been sucked out of his body, the patient is still not out of danger. The blighting witch has anticipated that his victim might be successful in obtaining effective aid and therefore, before leaving the neighborhood, has set up a secondary attack system in the form of another being from the spirit world. This one is called a *pasuk,* and it has the virtue of being able to launch the *tsentsak* as effectively as the witch himself.

For the purpose of this mission, the *pasuk* disguises itself as a harmless insect or common animal and lurks around the victim's house, watching for signs that he has been relieved of the original volley of *tsentsak*. As soon as the victim shows suspicious signs of a return to health, the *pasuk* hurls another flight of weapons into his body, causing a return of the initial symptoms.

The procedure is as classic as the introductory moves in a chess game. The healer has been half-expecting the relapse. He enters the spirit world through the usual door and sneaks up on his patient's house, reconnoitering cautiously. The *pasuk* is a dangerous foe. *Tsentsak* from the blighting witch cover its body like armor. Only its eyes are vulnerable.

As the healer readies for battle, his *tsentsak* cling tightly to him, watching for the inevitable volley; when it comes, like so many goalies in a hockey game, they prevent the weapon from scoring. For his part, the healer moves in closer and closer, waiting his chance. As soon as luck and skill give him a good shot at the *pasuk*'s eyes, he hurls a *tsentsak*, and if his aim is true, the *pasuk* falls dead at his feet.

Phase three of the duel begins quickly. The blighting witch calls up the services of a *wakani*, the dreaded spirit-bird. Arming the *wakani* with a few *tsentsak*, he sends it to the victim's house. This maneuver is the reverse of the earlier sneak attack. Screaming and hawking, the bird flies around the victim's head, launching weapon after weapon and terrifying the poor man to the point of madness. Sometimes the encounter sends the victim into shock from which he never recovers. If the man has steady nerves, the healing witch can again suck out the debilitating *tsentsak*, but the remedy is only temporary. The blighting witch sends the bird again and again, each time armed with a fresh supply of weapons. Each time the victim is left a little weaker than before. The only permanent cure is to destroy the *wakani*.

This particular spirit is especially clever at camouflage. The healer supplements *natema* with a draught of *maikua*, a powerful drink made from a species of the datura plant. The battle with the *wakani* is the denouement of the duel. If the healer kills the bird, his patient's recovery is assured. Even so, a careful healer stays with his patient until the following day. The patient's system has been corrupted by the long barrage of *tsentsak*. Additional therapy may be needed before all the sickness is removed.

The Jívaro do not know the art of shape-changing. However, they are able to use their associations in the spirit world to achieve many of the same functions medieval witches accomplished with shape-changing. The *anamuk* is a special type of spirit adept at assuming an animal shape in a convincing manner. If a witch were to attack and slay an enemy in his own person, reprisals from the dead man's relatives and tribe would be swift. As we have seen, homicide via *tsentsak* is often detected, and revenge customarily follows success. However, attack by an *anamuk* is often confused with a normal event of the jungle, and the real culprit is not suspect.

The Hindus say that in ancient India, which was the birthplace of Buddhism, the adherents of that religion were so successful in preaching the desirability of attaining nirvana that people abandoned the pains and pleasures of worldly life by the thousands and flocked to monastic life. So many people shaved their heads and took up the ochre robes of the monks that society almost starved for want of babies to carry on the work of their generation.

It would seem that the ease with which an individual can participate in mystic life through the comparatively simple process of drinking *natema* could easily result in a similar crisis. However, the Jívaro have built into the role conditions that make witchhood an insupportably extravagant profession, and an uncomfortable one as well. It is not an easy life. The powers they possess and the wonders they see come high.

The difficulties begin the moment a man determines to take up the profession. The Jívaro do not believe in public education. An experienced witch demands expensive gifts in return for the trouble of taking on a disciple. The expense is commensurate with the witch's proven ability.

Witchcraft is imparted from teacher to disciple by means of bestowing upon the novice some of the teacher's own *tsentsak*. Unprepared, they would destroy the novice. The first step is to introduce him to the practice of drinking *natema*. When that has been accomplished satisfactorily, the teacher, himself under the drug's influence, vomits up a vividly colored object that contains part of his legion of spirit helpers. With a single blow of his machete, he cuts off a corner of the object and hands it to the novice, who immediately swallows it.

The spirits are a strong force despite the *natema*, and their presence inside him makes him sick. For ten days he must rest in bed, drinking repeated doses of *natema* to strengthen his psychic powers so that he can contain the *tsentsak* in comfort. He is not alone during this painful and frightening period. His teacher makes frequent visits to his bedside, rubbing and blowing upon his body, an act that quiets the spirits and aids in the transfer. As soon as the novice is able, he may leave his bed, but for three months it is important that he remain inactive.

His most critical duty is also negative: he must avoid any sexual contact. If he is successful in this, at the end of the first month a *tsentsak* works its way up his throat and pops out of his mouth. This is a point of crisis. His future career rests on the outcome. The emerged *tsentsak* represents his first concrete powers as a witch. The sense of raw power and the spirit's combative influence combine to overwhelm him with a desire to murder. The itch nags at him day and night. It may be that the *tsentsak* of a blighting witch are especially vitriolic. Or it may be that the teacher's example is subtly persuasive. In any case, the disciples of a healing witch generally become healers, and the disciples of a blighting witch become blighting witches. However, this relationship is not foreordained.

Becoming a blighting witch requires no effort at all, but a healer must fight for his profession. If he can control the impulse to hurl that first *tsentsak*, he has won the battle. If he slips once, however, there is no going back, no way to make amends. By that single act, he has become a blighting witch for so long as he practices magic.

The direction of his destiny settled, the novice now begins to gather together his own fighting band of *tsentsak*. *Tsentsak* are rather like hermit crabs in their habits. They have no material bodies of their own; their being is pure spirit. Comfort seems to require that they put on a physical shell, so each *tsentsak* finds an object that appeals to it, enters the object, and takes up residency.

Only a witch can spot the spirits curled up within their borrowed homes. The novice obtains his spirits by gathering up their homes. Under the influence of *natema*, he is able to persuade them to come out of their hiding places and join up with him. The *tsentsak* are as many as the stars in the sky, yet each is unique, possessed of its own special powers. It takes perserverance and cleverness to discover and win them over. His future success, perhaps his very life, will depend on the pains he takes at this time.

This is equally true with regard to strict sexual abstinence. For his purposes, moderation or monogamy would be quite as bad as an orgy. Perhaps learning to control the spirits consumes all a man's energy. Whatever the reason, a novice must stay away from women for at least a year in order to perform adequately as a witch.

Finally, when he completes his novitiate of a year or more, his professional life expectancy is only five years. The duels he fights in the course of his career deplete his supply of *tsentsak*. As his supply of spirit helpers dwindles, his power to work magic weakens. And, throughout his career, whatever else he does, he must be careful not to anger his former teacher. At any time, the teacher can call back the original *tsentsak* that had formerly belonged to him and are now the foundation of the new witch's power.

The homing magic is a simple matter for the teacher. First, of course, he drinks *natema*. Then he has some of his *tsentsak* build a bridge of their essences, arched like a rainbow between him and his former disciple. The teacher takes a *tsentsak* and flings it along the bridge. The spirit strikes the earth near the disciple's feet, exploding with a roar and a blinding flash that confuse the disciple. Immediately, the teacher sucks back his original *tsentsak*.

This one act effectively strips the new witch of all his powers. If he is not aware of what has happened at the time of the explosion, he will discover it the next time he drinks *natema*. For the first time, the potion will not open the door to the spirit world for him. He will still be blind.

As the critical time of forced retirement draws near, or if he suddenly experiences a suspicious waning of his strength, he tests himself by attempting to split a tree in half by hurling his *tsentsak* at it. If he fails, he knows he no longer has the power to bewitch a human. Worse, he is now defenseless against the attack of another sorcerer.

The only means by which he can regain his powers is to go through another novitiate. However, the expense and privation involved often make him decide to let his profession slip away from him. The decision leaves him in a vulnerable state. He rests as much as possible to conserve such supernatural strength as is left to him, and he tries to conceal his new status from his enemies, who would be certain to attack if they knew the truth.

On the other hand, if he undergoes the effort once more, he knows his supernatural abilities are at the most on loan, and at the end of five years the power and the glory will be gone.

Drugs are a basic tool in sorcery. It is doubtful that a witch ever lived and practiced that did not occasionally avail himself of a chemical assist to his inner occult powers. The Jívaro witches are at the far end of the distribution curve in this characteristic. It is difficult to imagine drugs being used more frequently in witchcraft than they use them. In fact, the question arises whether the five-year cutoff might not represent the average witch's physical tolerance to such large quantities of drugs consumed over long periods of time. Certainly, a bout of sorcery leaves healer and blighting witch alike depleted of energy. The decision to leave witchcraft may well reflect increasing physiological difficulties as well as financial and emotional ones, and be the hidden price of acquiring occult vision.

The Jívaro witches are unusual in their candor about the intricacies of their magic. This, too, may stem from their almost complete reliance on chemicals as a bridge to the spirit world. Their sorcery, operating with the automatism of a wet-cell battery, is lean on discipline and mystery, requiring only the price of a starter of *tsentsak* for admission.

CHAPTER SIX

The Lady of Witches

The similarity of witchcraft around the world is almost frightening. One expects differences to match the differences in language, food, clothing, and custom.

The patterns of witchcraft are as basic as the patterns of human life and death. It is as though witches drew their magic from a common pool of supernatural knowledge. Witchcraft that is currently being practiced throughout South America, Central America, and Mexico bears a strong resemblance to what we know of medieval European witchcraft. Modern historians claim this is due either to coincidence or to information the Indians picked up from Spanish conquistadores and passed down from generation to generation.

Perhaps.

There is no question that the Spanish adventurers brought their sorcery with them to help in the giant task of plundering the strange new country they had discovered. In fact, many of the soldiers had boarded ship only a half-step ahead of the pursuing Inquisition because, in the face of torture and death, they had continued in their old beliefs.

Still, it may be a mistake to consider natural means the only method of transmitting supernatural wisdom. Witchcraft flourished in the Americas before Cortes. Before Columbus. Before Christ.

Most of it has been lost. The Spaniards destroyed the greater part of the Indian learning which they encountered in the name of God. Before the Spaniards, the competing tribes had also wiped out great sections of each other's supernatural wisdom as it was captured, in the name of military expediency: stripped of this knowledge a people would be powerless. Temples, libraries, and priests, all were destroyed. Only the gods remained, but they were served by the conqueror's own priests and so became their gods.

It is difficult for someone raised in a Christian country to imagine the extent to which religion and magic merged among the peoples of what is now lower Mexico, Guatemala, Salvador, and Honduras, and the extent to which both permeated their everyday lives.

According to these people, the gods and goddesses themselves practiced witchcraft. The greatest magician among the gods was called the Lady of Witches and was the shape-changing goddess Tlazolteotl. The Aztec artists left a number of images of her. Wearing a crown of raw cotton and seated on a broomstick, she looked surprisingly similar to portraits of medieval witches on their way to a sabbat.

Like the Jívaro, the Aztecs did not reject blighting witchcraft but channeled these talents into projects benefiting the state. Montezuma II sent a band of blighting witches to Cortes with instructions to curse him. They were unable to complete their mission because a turncoat Aztec girl attached to Cortes became suspicious of them and warned the soldiers to turn them away.

Even rogue witches willing to kill and injure those of their own villages were not considered outlaws by the Aztecs. Death was the normal climax of life, sickness a counterpart to health, and blighting magic, like storms, part of nature.

Even gods and goddesses have their times of strength and their times of weakness. All created things come and go. The Aztecs believed their nation, like themselves and like the powerful Toltec nation before it, having been born, would one day wither into nothingness. Magical threats to the individual or the nation were fought with counter-magic, but not with an attitude of self-righteousness or self-pity.

Robber sorcery is the one instance of witchcraft that was rejected by society. By obtaining the forearm and hand of a woman who had died giving birth to her first child, a thief could do his work at minimum risk. Waved before the doorway of the house, the dismembered limb cast a deep sleep upon the inhabitants. The Aztecs saw these robber-sorcerers as great criminals, not because they used magic to interfere with another's freedom of action, but because they took the fruits of another's labor, an act that was akin to stealing his time, stealing a precious bit of the man's life. Further, and perhaps more important, the theft robbed the Aztec nation of its good name.

The Aztecs confined their righteousness to matters of ritual obligation. In this their punitive obsessiveness may have been a reflection more of frantic necessity than moral indignation. For the Aztecs, worship was pragmatic rather than romantic. They gave to the gods and goddesses so that they would be given gifts in return. It was almost a matter of an eye for an eye, a tooth for a tooth. They gave the gods life, countless human lives, so that the gods would give them life.

The Aztec religious calendar was set to the rhythm of human sacrifice. In some seasons, the heart was pulled out of the living body and offered still pulsing and spurting blood; in other seasons, the skin was flayed bit by bit off the flesh; at yet another time the head was struck from the shoulders. In these sacrifices, the Aztecs were offering up the best their nation had to give. They believed that the god to whom the sacrifice was made entered the body of his offering. In anticipation of this occurrence, the person to be sacrificed was dressed in the clothing of the god and often, though not always, went joyfully to his fate. Enemy captives were offered up to the war gods on a share-the-loot basis, for without the gods the victory would have been impossible.

With the former type of sacrifice, after the offering had been made, the victim's body was cut into small pieces and eaten by the celebrants and all the worshippers as an act of communion. As we have seen, this type of communion is frequently associated with witchcraft.

In the early part of Aztec history, the number of sacrifices was small. But as they felt their cycle coming to a close, the sacrifices became prodigious, as though it required more and more of an effort on their part to obtain a satisfactory response from the gods. To supplement the sacrifice of life, the Aztecs made demi-offerings of blood and pain, piercing tongues and ears with pointed bone awls or cactus spines at regular intervals.

Every person sacrificed. However, it was felt that the sacrifice which secular people were capable of making and still continuing with their daily work was inadequate to meet the need. The main function of the Aztec priesthood was to ensure an unending flow of human pain and blood from the nation to the gods. The life of an Aztec priest, like that of a Catholic saint, consisted of asceticism and suffering. Any error, however slight, in the ritual of sacrifice or in any ceremonial nullified the results they were endeavoring to achieve.

Eroticism, that persuasive distraction, was considered sinful and dangerous to priest and layman alike. Copulation, except in rigidly structured situations, was forbidden. Adultery and premarital sexual intercourse were punished by stoning.

Nevertheless, the witch goddess Tlazolteotl delighted in sexual activity. She had the power to seduce the gods themselves. Some of the legends say the great and pure Quetzalcoatl had a love affair with her. The unfortunate mortal male whom it amused her to ensnare with passion was helpless against her.

Tlazolteotl was the patron of the blighting witches. A goddess of many moods, faces, and even ages, her devotees also had mastery over their bodies, being able to assume animal forms at will. Rather than the evil eye, Aztec witches had evil fingers, infecting an enemy's body with foreign substances by the act of pointing.

Also dedicated to her service were the beautiful young women who were kept to satisfy the sexual needs of the soldiers. Their mouths were painted black as an insignia of their unique role in Aztec life. Dressed and perfumed to excite the soldiers, they practiced their arts for a few short years and then were sacrificed to the soldiers' patron, Tezcatlipoca.

Death by sacrifice was appropriate for those who served the witch-goddess, who watched over suffering and was often pictured in a dress made of the skin of a sacrifice. She is shown in the act of giving birth to a younger version of herself. The symbol of the younger goddess was the moon; that of the older form of the goddess was the severed head and streaming heart of a young man.

The degree to which the Aztecs felt blighting magic to be the other side of the coin of curing magic, and evil the normal counterpart of good, is shown by the double nature of the goddess. For if the Lady of the Witches was the queen of evil, lust, and suffering, she was also the goddess of forgiveness; *Eater of Filth,* the Aztecs called her in that mood. The broom on which she rides she used to sweep away the sins of mankind. The temple-girls that were given to the soldiers were spoken of as "Tlazolteotl's brooms," the devices used by the soldiers to keep their minds free of sexual thoughts at times inappropriate to such things.

Once in the life of every man, Tlazolteotl was willing to sweep him free of sin and evil if he went through the proper ceremony of pain in her honor. The man who had reached middle life, when the passions of youth were somewhat under control, and who wished to be freed of his former sins, would seek out one of Tlazolteotl's priests. As though he were speaking to the goddess herself, he would make a full confession to him, beginning with his first occasion of sin and continuing from transgression to transgression until he had touched upon every sin committed throughout his life.

When he had finished his confession, the priest would describe what he had to do. He must refuse to eat for four days. On the last night of his fast, he must strip off his clothes except for a little apron hugging his loins. Kneeling, he would pierce his tongue with the spine of a cactus and pull a length of straw all the way through the wound. Similarly, he must pierce his tongue with another spine and pull a straw through that wound. Discarding that straw, he must draw straw after straw until a mound of eight hundred of them lay at his feet.

When the ceremony was complete, Tlazolteotl, the same goddess who had inflamed his senses and beguiled his reason when he was young, would forgive and cleanse him.

However, he must sin no more. Absolution comes but once.

Tlazolteotl was not the only divinity who practiced sorcery. Tezcatlipoca, the god of the soldiers, was a great magician. His name, *Mirror that Smokes*, linked him to the priestly art of foreseeing the future by looking into the great black obsidian mirror. Like Tlazolteotl, he had a double nature. One of his names meant *He Who Stands at the Shoulder*. He would sneak up on each man, whispering into his ear, coaxing him to forget ritual and formality, to yield to caprice and folly. Yet Tezcatlipoca gave Tlazolteotl the broom she used to sweep away sin.

As befits a warrior-god, he loved bravery and used his magic to reward the courageous. At night, in his form of the Jeweled Turkey, he would make his strange gobbling cry. If the man who heard the sound ran up and seized the god, holding on to him despite the terror of his cries and the awful aspect of his face, he would receive great wealth. But if the man gave in to fear and fled, the god struck away his reason; the man was doomed to spend the rest of his years as a gibbering idiot.

The priests followed the gods' example in making full use of magic. In a very real sense, the Aztec nation was ruled by sorcery.

Even the emperor, who was a secular ruler and a

soldier, and was considered to be the living embodiment of the Aztec people, practiced divination as part of his duties. Many of the priests were mediums, conversing with the spirit world from the depths of their trances. Even a non-priest would, from time to time, be seized by a god to be used in passing along some communication.

All of the priests, from the highest to the lowest, were trained in astronomy, numerology, herbology, and magical ritual. All practiced the power-giving rites of pain. All were trained to chew peyotl buttons and smeared their bodies with ointment made from the ololiuqui vine (*Rivea corymbosa*). Many of the details of their sorcery were learned in drug-induced visions.

In addition to the solar calendar that the practical Aztecs used for agriculture, their priests devised another calendar based on a lost system of numerology for the purpose of divining the future and regulating their magical rites. The system was too intricate to trust to memory. It was written down in their Books of Magic and kept in trust for the use of the entire nation. These books were so explicit that even priests who lacked the ability to deal with the higher mysteries of their calling could function as fortune tellers for the peasants. Each village had its priest–fortune teller who advised the people on such specific matters as when to plan a trip, go hunting, marry, or go to the market.

The high magic the head priests practiced is lost. We know that their duties were directed toward manipulating the gods as a method of influencing the weather and the fortune of the Aztec nation.

However, the priests' prowess in foreseeing the future convinced them that the gods, like nature, were bound on a wheel of destiny against which no magic was effective. The essence that was beyond the wheel of destiny, beyond the gods' and the sorcerers' power, they called Ometecuhtli, the Unknowable. The cycles of nature, the rhythms of life, the essence of duality originated in him. Since he was immovable, unknowable, beyond both experience and influence, they built no temples to him, offered no sacrifices, attempted no visions of him. By the use of their magic, some of his cycles could be foreknown—the birth and death of an individual, of a town, a field, a nation—but they could not be altered. Ometecuhtli was not loved by the priests, and he was not feared; he was accepted.

The common people, the farmers, artisans, and merchants who were the life-sustaining force of the nation, practiced low magic dedicated to the practicalities of everyday life, especially to healing. Village healers were as likely to be women as men. The potions, ointments, rites, and copious sweat baths they prescribed were designed to bring the patient into harmony with nature. And nature, to them, encompassed both the material world and the invisible supernatural world of the gods, goddesses, and spirits. The healers used peyote and mushrooms in order to consult with the gods about the proper diagnosis and treatment of their patients.

Judging from the behavior of the Spanish soldiers, this approach to healing was effective. Officially, of course, the Spaniards were bound to maintain that the Aztec healers were spawn of the devil. Unofficially, however, they soon abandoned their own doctors and surgeons for the superior care they received from the Aztecs.

Aztec witchcraft is exciting in itself, and as a background for the sorcery that is being practiced in

Guatemala and Mexico today it is invaluable. It has the additional asset of demonstrating that a culture not devil- and sin-oriented can, nevertheless, maintain a highly disciplined life based not on guilt but on pragmatism.

CHAPTER SEVEN

Healing and Blighting

New World witchcraft has shown more vitality than New World religion. It has survived the Catholic church. Whether it will also survive Cokes, assembly-line production, and mass media remains to be seen.

The high magic of the Aztecs died with the priests who practiced it. They were few, belligerent to the Spaniards, fiercely nationalistic, and powerfully influential among their people. The Spaniards killed them. But the common people, of course, were too useful to be killed. Furthermore, it was not really necessary. Being conquered was familiar to them. Fortunately for their peace of mind, the church's priests were not aware that the religion they were forcing upon the people at swordpoint had many elements in common with the old religion: the duty to offer pain to God, communion involving the act of eating the flesh of God, the sinfulness of non-marital sex, the legion of saints with their pragmatic duties. The people were able to make the transfer of obedience from their former soldiers and priests to the Spanish soldiers and

81

priests without too much readjustment, however reluctant they were to do so.

Their witchcraft, the witchcraft of the sorcerers and healers, the people kept. And all the threats and rages and entreaties of their new priests could not persuade them to let go of it. This witchcraft is still practiced with great enthusiasm and conviction in Central America, Mexico, and parts of California, Texas, and Arizona. It differs somewhat from European sorcery and is only a fragment of the knowledge the Aztec nation had at its disposal. Still, supernatural wisdom has amazing elasticity. Even truncated and made alien, the rhythm of witchcraft is always similar and its goal is the same: to keep the man, physical nature, and the supernatural functioning in harmony. Witches may well supply guidelines to replace the instincts that man has lost and other animals still possess. Although their means are not a part of reality as philosophy instructors know it, in a deeper sense their powers come from nature.

In Guatemala, due to centuries-long contact with the Catholic church, the categories of healing and blighting witches have become somewhat blurred. The *brujo* is unequivocally a blighting witch and very much feared. Then there are two types of evil-doers who are not regarded as witches but who belong to the realm of the supernatural.

The two practitioners of benevolent sorcery are not so easy to place. *Zorines* can see into the future. Generally, they are a positive force within the community, handing out excellent advice on important matters of family concern, business, and agriculture. However, they are known to have quick tempers, and in moments of anger they may turn the force of their hostile magic against someone. Neither are the healing witches, the *curanderos* or *parcheros,* entirely trusted.

The differences in the relationship between community and witch for the Jívaro and the peasants of Guatemala illustrate the disservice society does to itself by making hostile witchcraft illegal.

Among the Jívaro, blighting and curing witches are on the same team and working for the same goal, each in his special fashion. Other witches have also been known to show remarkable national loyalty. The late Gerald Brousseau Gardiner, a famous contemporary English witch, told the story of the English witches who gathered on Lammas Day in 1940 and slowly raised a great cone of power which they directed toward Hitler. Then the conjuration was uttered: "You cannot cross the sea. You cannot come. You cannot come." Many witches died in the effort of throwing their vital forces into that act; others were invalided; but none of them will ever forget or ever regret being a part of that sorcery.

In Guatemala, the dictum that *brujos* serve the devil and are accursed is accepted. The effect has been the same as that of loosing a group of cancer cells in the bloodstream of a living body. Their illegal status has not lessened their number, but since society has placed them outside its formal structure, they are not bound by its jurisdiction. Independent and isolated, the *brujos* feel free to attack anyone as whim or payment dictates. And the hostility directed toward them makes them increasingly spiteful. The lives of the villagers are spent in fear of malicious witchcraft. If they anger anyone in the village, he is apt to pay a *brujo* to bewitch them.

Pedro had a fight with his neighbor about an unruly goat; the neighbor sought out a *brujo*. Don Tomás had three years of good luck with his crops; one of his friends took his envy to the witch. Guadelupe and her husband fought with a cousin over some land; the cousin tried to destroy both of them through sorcery.

This terrible, ever-present fear eats away at the happiness of village life, driving the individual away from the comfort and solidarity of the group to isolation and loneliness.

Suspicion is the prevailing mood of the villagers. Each of them walks in as much fear of being accused of sorcery as he does of being bewitched himself. Social dissolution has reached the point where a man does not dare watch his friend's pottery being baked, because if the vessels come out black from the flames, he will be accused of being responsible for the imperfections.

This kind of distrust corrodes affection among members of the immediate family as well. Children have been known to engage a *brujo* to attack their parents. Wives have hired *brujos* against their husbands. There is no one with whom an individual can feel absolutely safe.

The *brujos* and their customers are for the most part an invisible enemy, but some of the blighting witches have been identified and are looked upon with fear, hatred, and awe. However, like the criminals they are, most of them manage to keep their actual business a secret. Their customers come to them in the dark of night when there is no moon. A man will not give the name of a *brujo* to another unless he is sure he will use his services and so make them accomplices. A *brujo*'s customers are hated and avoided by the villagers as much as the witch himself.

The arts of the *brujo* are thought to be acquired. However, the witch will only take as an apprentice someone he feels has a calling for the profession. The skills he will learn are impressive. Like the Aztec sorcerers, he can cause sickness by introducing foreign substances into the body of a victim. *Brujos* have lost the trick of doing this by pointing, so today's witches go through a lengthy procedure called "burying the doll." They can regulate the degree of sickness they wish to produce by varying the substance to be projected into the person. Worms, for example, are more uncomfortable than dangerous. On the other hand, conjuring a small animal inside the victim's belly will eventually kill him. The doll, an effigy of the victim, can be programmed in other ways. Drenching it with cold water will infect the victim with influenza; torturing it with pins and then burying it will result in a painful death.

Brujos can also cause sickness by dictating the content of a victim's dream. Making a man dream he has been charged by a puma or jaguar or bitten by a snake produces results in twenty-four hours.

Although *brujos* are isolated from the world of men by their profession, they are not alone. Hordes of evil spirits befriend them. Thanks to these friends, the witches do not lack for women. The spirits give the *brujos* the secret of invisibility, which allows them to sneak into a man's house at night and enjoy his woman without detection.

Lichus or *lechuza* is the name given to men born with the ability to turn into a bird and fly. It is hard to know whether the talent predestines such a man to a life of theft or whether only the thieves are found out. They are such powerful magicians that they are able to steal from a *brujo* without fear of sickness. But they do have one point of vulnerability. Their spirits must assume the form of birds, and while they are flying through the sky, their bodies lie unguarded below.

There is the story of Pablo Larraz, for instance, who lived better than most of the men in his village but did much less work. First there was talk about him; then there was watching. One night late, he was seen to sneak out of his house. Stealthily, he dodged from shadow to shadow until he had reached the fields outside his village. His neighbors followed and saw him lie down in a clump of tall grass that would ordinarily conceal him. As they watched, they saw a large bird fly out of his mouth and flap away.

After half an hour the bird had not returned. The neighbors worked up the courage to approach Pablo Larraz. He was lying on the ground, his eyes shut, his mouth gaping open. His flesh felt as cold as though he were lying in his coffin.

His neighbors went back to their hiding place and continued their vigil. When the sky had lightened to a midnight blue, the bird came flying back with something in its beak: a fat stack of pesos. The bird dropped the pesos in Pablo Larraz's hand, crawled into his mouth, and disappeared.

The next day, the neighbors went around the village inquiring whether anyone had lost any money. Sure enough, a *milpero* complained that during the night a thief had taken the money he had been saving for the *fiesta titular*.

The next time the neighbors saw Pablo Larraz sneaking out of his house at midnight, they followed him again. They waited until the bird emerged from his mouth and flew away. Then they went over to Pablo Larraz and turned his body so that his mouth was pressed securely against the earth. When the bird came back, it flapped frantically around and around his head, but it could not find a way to enter the mouth. After an hour, it flew off slowly.

Pablo Larraz was dead.

Even though the story of Pablo Larraz was recited

with approval, as an example of just punishment awarded to a rogue, the *lechuzas* are not feared and hated as the *brujos* are. It is felt that the *lechuzas* are cursed with their power, and at least their magic is not directed against human flesh.

Magic can be cured only by magic. No matter how greatly the villagers distrust the *zahorines*, the *curanderos*, and the *parcheros*, they must go to them for help when they have been struck down by a witch. They make the best of a bad situation by hiring a healer from another town, on the grounds that a stranger will at least be neutral.

Sadly enough, the healers themselves feel guilty about practicing magic in opposition to the church's injunctions. They go to great lengths to draw Christ, his mother, and the saints into their rituals. Christian prayers and offerings accompany their conjurations. The healer interrupts his cure to explain to the Holy Family why the procedure is necessary and to beg their approval of his magic.

This uneasy juxtaposition of witchcraft and religion is reminiscent of the situation in Europe in the eleventh century, and suggests the danger that the villagers of Guatemala may erupt in a fever of witch hunting. It would be one way to rid themselves of the fear and guilt oppressing them. Unfortunately, it would leave an emptiness that urban education has not demonstrated it can fill.

Watching a healer at work is an impressive sight. A typical instance came about when Luis, a charcoal maker, found himself unable to perform his usual duties. He believed a *brujo* had cursed him. His mother feared he had been afflicted with the evil eye. A friend persuaded him that whatever the cause, his only help would come from a *curandero*. Reluctantly, Luis put out the money to bring a well-known *curandero* to his village from a neighboring town to treat him.

After the *curandero* had chatted informally with Luis for a while, he began his examination by staring into the sick man's eyes. When he had finished with this, he withdrew into himself for a while; then he informed Luis that he was sick because he had sustained a *susto*.

Susto, or supernatural fright, does not result from a curse. However, it is fully as dangerous as being cursed. The problem arises because the soul flees in terror from the body. Without his soul, Luis's body had sickened. Unless his soul was restored, he would die.

First it was necessary to determine what had given Luis the *susto*. The *curandero* discovered that by looking into his patient's eyes. He told Luis that the fright had come about when he overheard his brother, Miguel, lying about him to their parents.

Sobbing, Luis confirmed the *curandero*'s diagnosis. He had overheard his brother using falsehoods to create an estrangement between him and his mother and father. As he listened, he had felt a cold fear that his parents would disinherit him and give the grove of oak trees they had promised him to Miguel. His brother had often said that he should receive the larger part of their parents' land because he was the older son. Worse than that, his father appeared to love only Miguel. Now Luis was convinced that his father would leave him nothing and he would never be able to hold up his head as a landowner.

The *curandero* listened to the young man's story in silence. When it was done, he told Luis he would accept the case only if his directions were followed to the last detail. Luis agreed to this condition.

Over Luis's protests, the *curandero* told the parents in detail the events leading up to the young man's sickness. After the parents had been given some time to think the matter over, he instructed Luis to go to them and ask them to help him in the curing ceremony. They agreed gladly. The *curandero* then gave the family a list of preparations to be made for the ceremony, which he announced would take place in five days.

Luis and his father were busy from sunup to dark searching the fields beyond the village for the herbs and roots the *curandero* needed. Luis's mother was equally busy preparing the fiesta the *curandero* had told her to provide for the family, its relatives, and their friends, all of whom were to be invited to the ceremony. Even Miguel began helping in the preparations for Luis's cure.

On the fifth day, a Tuesday, when the sun was low on the horizon, the guests arrived. Luis was lying on his bed looking pale and nervous. The *curandero* arrived and congratulated the family on the decorations they had put up for the fiesta. He was presented to the guests and spoke with each for a few minutes.

The *curandero* then selected three of Luis's most important relatives, deputizing them to go to the village cathedral and light candles for the success of the enterprise and to kneel before the altar of Luis's patron saint, telling him of the young man's dire condition and the importance of the curing ceremony, and begging the saint to intercede on behalf of their efforts.

After the three had left, the *curandero* selected a copal incense burner from among the items Luis and his father had obtained for him and went himself, walking slowly with bowed head, to the cathedral. He lit some candles for the success of his cure and then, waving his incense burner, walked over to the main altar, kneeling to explain to Mary in great detail the cause of Luis's *susto* and plead with her to take a motherly interest in the sick boy.

When the *curandero* returned to the house, he told Luis to rise from his cot and stand before the household altar. Selecting an egg from the items he had requested, the *curandero* rubbed it over the right side of Luis's body from the crown of his head to the genitalia. Then he selected a second egg and used it to rub the left side of Luis's body.

He placed the two eggs in a basket and told Miguel, the brother, to position the basket on the exact spot outside the door of the house where Luis had been standing when he overheard the *susto*-producing conversation. The *curandero* knelt before the household altar and lit a candle. He told the Virgin that the two eggs had absorbed the wicked winds that had invaded Luis's body after he had lost his soul. He told the Virgin that he had caused the eggs to be placed on the spot where the soul had been lost in the hopes that the evil spirits who now had charge of it would see the suffering and pain the winds had caused and be overcome with pity for the boy.

The *curandero* demanded next that all the lights of the household be extinguished except the candle he had lit at the altar. He ordered the guests to kneel in prayer. Then he and Miguel went outside, taking with them two candles, a rope of cigars, a jug of *pulque*, some sweets, cacao seeds, some parrot feathers that had been sown together, and a bundle of herbs.

The *curandero* knelt at the spot where Miguel had placed the eggs. He lit the candles and began praying to the spirits in a loud voice. Under his direction, Miguel had dug a large hole in the ground. The *curandero* now took two small images from his pocket and placed them next to the hole. Then, detailing the virtues of each gift, he placed them all, one by one, in the hole in front of the images. He went over the entire story of the *susto* again, offering the eggs as evidence that what he said was true. He reminded the spirits that they had known him for a long time and that he had done many favors for them in the past and had always honored them and heaped upon them many rich gifts. Now, he said, he came to them asking a favor. He begged them to find the soul of Luis and to restore it to his body before the wicked winds again invaded it with more sickness and suffering. The *curandero* placed the eggs in the hole on top of the gifts and covered them all with dirt.

Returning to the house, the *curandero* then lit two more candles at the household altar. He beckoned Luis to follow him and led the young man outside to the spot where he had sustained his *susto*. Lighting four candles, he placed one of them in each of the four cardinal directions, kneeling facing each direction and praying aloud as he placed each candle.

Next the *curandero* took a potion Miguel and the boy's father had concocted at his direction, consisting of ground herbs, roots, and seeds dissolved in alcohol brewed from the aguave cactus. The *curandero* ordered Luis to take off his clothes. As the young man, flushing violently, pulled down his pants, the *curandero* covered his genitalia with a cloth apron. Embarrassed and shivering with cold, Luis stood while the *curandero* recited a long conjuration in an Indian dialect.

The *curandero* had Luis take three long drinks of the potion. As the boy sipped, he recited another conjuration. When Luis had finished, the *curandero* held up the bowl containing the tincture as though he were about to make an offering. Then, moving with deliberate speed, he poured the potion over Luis's head, letting it drip down his shoulders, back, and chest and fall in rivulets down his legs.

The alcohol in the potion increased Luis's shivering to violent shaking. Luis complained, asking to be allowed to dry off. Sternly, the *curandero* ordered him to be silent. He led the boy inside the house and had him stretch out in front of the household altar. He took up a basket of eggs and began rubbing them, one by one, over Luis's body. Only then did he allow the young man to dress and get back into bed.

The *curandero* heaped blankets on Luis. He ordered Miguel to put a pot of warm coals under the bed. The *curandero* crawled under the bed, passing his hands over the coals. Flames shot up and a strong pungent odor filled the room. *"La espirita esta aqui,"* the *curandero* said with quiet satisfaction.

Then he picked up the eggs he had used to rub Luis's body, breaking them into a bowl of water. He peered at the eggs in silence for a long time. Finally, he looked up, declaring that the cure had been successful. The wicked winds had left the boy's body, and new winds had replaced them. Now that the soul was back, all would soon be well.

The ceremony had taken most of the night. Luis did not wake up until late the next day. Even then, he was drowsy and untalkative. However, within the week he was up and doing his chores, as healthy as ever. Furthermore, Luis and his family were on closer and more affectionate terms than they had been for some time.

CHAPTER EIGHT

The Evil Eye

When members of the *Raza*, the Mexican people, came to the United States, they brought their *curanderos* with them. Their need was great, for their adopted country was interested in the amount of labor it could extract from them, not in their well-being.

As time went on, more and more members of the *Raza* made a place for themselves in this country, had their children here, and became Americans as well as Mexicans. Eventually, this group grew large and strong enough to exert pressure on the appropriate governmental agencies and force them to take some interest in the welfare of Mexican-Americans, many of whom are having economic difficulties.

As a result of this action and various employer-participant medical plans, increasing numbers of Mexican-Americans have been exposed to big clinic medicine. But those that have not, and a surprising number of those that have, still seek out a *curandero*. Again and again, Mexican-Americans have complained that the sterile procedures of contemporary medicine are ineffectual against their illnesses. Gringos whose business it is to observe them have confirmed that this is the case. Often, embarrassed gringo case workers, school teachers, and even some perceptive doctors have had to encourage their clients to seek out *curanderos*, because in their experience that is what gets the job done.

This is not to deny the excellent work accomplished by medicine: its pharmacology, the skill of its surgeons, the supereye of the microscope, the uses of radiology, the new methods of splinting bones, and much more. However, there is something lacking in medicine, something that was lost when the discipline broke away from witchcraft. Something whose lack many progressive physicians decry but cannot seem to replace.

Perhaps it is a wild talent that witches trained and exploited. Call it empathy, call it telepathy, or call it divination, in healing it functions as the ability to know what is wrong with the patient as a man and to treat him as a whole person, not merely to dabble with the symptoms affecting a portion of his body.

Reports of the evil eye come from all parts of the globe. Its prevalence among the *Raza* suggests that the pre-Cortez civilizations of Mexico and Central America were familiar with the phenomenon. In Europe, it is generally thought to be exercised as a voluntary talent. Among the contemporary peoples of Mexico and Central America, on the other hand, it is thought of as a relatively rare inherited capacity that operates in an automatic fashion sometimes contrary to its possessor's conscious intent.

In fact, a person born with the evil eye may not even be aware that he possesses it. Like Typhoid Mary, he goes his way obliviously creating havoc. The hidden power is triggered by the slightest passing touch of envy in its possessor. The peasants of Guatemala suffer from the effects of the evil eye, but there the problem is overshadowed by the greater one of the *brujo*. In this country, the menace is aggravated because the communal environment promotes envy.

An on-going conflict exists between the *Raza* and the alien culture that surrounds them; and within the Mexican-American community there is also conflict between the conservatives who want to preserve their cultural identity and the restless young people who want to become fully "Americanized." Generally, the conservatives maintain their ancient customs at the price of material success and have little money and few possessions. On the other hand, although the rebels are more successful financially, they lose the support of the group and are denied a sense of belonging.

Two centuries after the death of the Aztec nation, the *Raza* persist in the belief that the misdeeds of a single member of the group harm the people as a whole. Since they are devout Christians, the modern form of this idea is that the delinquent makes God angry at them rather than that it excites the wrath of one or more of the Aztec pantheon of deities; but the feeling of the mystical union of responsibility remains unchanged. This belief contributes to the anxiety of Mexican-Americans, because in this country they have no way of enforcing the code of the *Raza*.

The frustration resulting from the absence of legal power is intense, for the attitudes of the surrounding culture and those of the *Raza* are often diametrically opposed. As they see it, money, notoriety, and self-seeking independence are the important values in this country. Their tradition emphasizes loyalty to and love of family, religious devotion, and wisdom.

Such a conflict thrusts temptation upon every Mexican-American. All of them, especially the young, are exposed daily to the inimical values whenever they leave the house or let the outside world in, whether in the form of mass media communication or of a gringo visitor. Inevitably, some succumb. Of those that do, some disappear in the alien sea, becoming *agringados,* those who live like or even pretend to be gringos. Most of the rebels spend their days acting like gringos and their nights being Mexican. Members of both groups cause grief and a sense of impending danger to their families and to the *Raza* at large. There still remains a bedrock of those, generally old and often poor, who are uncontaminated by the gringo world and are a source at once of strength and annoyance to the others.

Such an atmosphere breeds supernatural sickness. The evil eye hits the Mexican-American community hard.

Fortunately, the effects are not fatal. They are merely uncomfortable, damaging, and often unattractive. Children are especially vulnerable to the evil eye. Their very purity and beauty excites envy, and their innocence makes them vulnerable to such an attack. Great precautions are taken to see that no stranger has contact with a newborn baby. When the child reaches school age, the mother experiences unease in sending him off to possible danger. If he develops a bad rash, if he cannot sleep at night, the parents know the evil eye has struck. They begin the task of trying to recall the names of people who have had contact with him.

Treatment is easier if the person who cast the evil eye cooperates in undoing the harm he has caused. All that is needed is that he touch the child. That instant of body contact negates the power his envious gaze exerted over the child.

When the possessor of the evil eye cannot be found or is believed to be a gringo, the *curandero* is called. Customarily, the *curandero* will rub an egg over the baby's body for the purpose of allowing the white of the egg to absorb the negative force. The ritual is similar to the one that cured Luis of his *susto*. Following this, the *curandero* will further purify the baby by carefully brushing it with a bundle of herbs.

The anesthesia and bed rest available in the maternity wards of medical clincs are enticing increasing numbers of Mexican-American women to avail themselves of their services. These mothers feel guilty about permitting themselves to be hospitalized because, although the delivery is easier for them in the hospital, their babies are exposed to possible contamination from the evil eye. Frequently, as soon as the baby is brought home the parents will ask the *curandero* to conduct the ceremony, even though the baby has not shown any symptoms of the disease.

Adults can be injured by the evil eye as well as children. Nothing is safe from attack: animals, plants, and inanimate objects can be damaged in this way. Brides have been disfigured by uncharacteristic acne on their wedding days. Young men's cars have unaccountably broken down. Whole batches of Christmas tamales have been ruined. Young hens have suddenly stopped laying eggs. Fine-looking patches of corn have failed to kernel up properly. Young boys have complained that in the midst of a game their favorite shooter has suddenly split in two.

None of these events can be described as major tragedies. Nevertheless, they make it evident that the possessor of the evil eye is not popular in the community, regardless of the pains he may take to nullify his blighting power. Often, he feels himself accursed. He can minimize the rejection he encounters only by taking meticulous care where his eyes fall and by touching any person or object he finds himself admiring.

Mexican-Americans report that whites and blacks are equally likely to be afflicted with the power, and that they find the incidence among these groups as frequent as among themselves. Surprisingly, this sharing of a common affliction causes only dissension between the Mexican-Americans and the other groups. Blacks and whites alike are insulted when they are told they have the evil eye and refuse to cooperate in negating its effects.

It is not possible to teach a person through a book to detect the presence of the evil eye when he encounters it. The evil eye escapes the still photographer's shutter as well. Possibly a motion picture camera could capture the glance that curses. A group of undergraduates at a large western university has been toying with the notion of undertaking such an experimental project. But the best way to learn to detect the evil eye is to go to someone who can identify it and learn from him. It does not take long. The response seems to be kinetic. A muscle spasm in the gut, a thrill, or a tremor occurs in the presence of the evil eye. Of course, that may be a secondary reaction. Some people report that they experience the spasm in the buttocks or the elbows.

In this country, the *curandero* is accepted more whole-heartedly than in Guatemala. It may be that, in contrast to the areligious approach to healing taken by medical doctors, the *curandero*'s obvious devotion to God outweighs the dubious sources of his power.

In this country, the magical source of the *curandero*'s healing power is effectively ignored. The power is spoken of as coming from God. Hence, Mexican-Americans perceive no need to apologize to God for availing themselves of the *curandero*'s services. On the contrary, they feel they are fulfilling their duty to God by going to the *curandero* instead of to the clinics where the doctors do not care about matters of faith. They are not suprised to find that those who ignore God will also lie. The medical doctors pretend that they can cure the illness of the evil eye and the *susto* even though they can't, while the *curandero* will send his clients to the clinic if that is what is best for them.

The *curanderos* have enlarged their methods of treatment to include practices which in this country are legal only for medical doctors. In Arizona, a woman healer who illegally dispenses drugs from a one-room office in a two-story stucco building explained her position:

"You must understand, there are two types of disease, natural disease and disease of the spirit. With natural disease, it is good to use any natural means to restore the body's inner harmony. Sweat baths are good. Antibiotics are also good if that is what is needed. When the hot wound of a farm hand is swollen with pus, when a young man has gone astray and has a sickness in his sex organs, I give them antibiotic. Thyroid and insulin are also good if the body is out of balance and cannot provide enough for its use. I give these things to my clients, God does the rest.

"There is no difficulty in obtaining medicines. Every three months I go to Mexico and bring them back with me. There is less difficulty in knowing when to use them. The message is written on the flesh of the person who is sick. And God helps me read the message. Administering the medicine is easy. A baby can use a hypodermic syringe. The difficulty comes if you get caught. The American judges are hard and cruel."

This *curandera* accused American doctors of growing rich on the sores of the bodies of their patients. "In this town," she said, "they would let you die on the front steps of their hospital if you have no money. I care for people whether they have money or not. I do not tell them what to give me. They give what they can. Really, it is not to me they give, but to the Virgin. I have them leave their offerings in front of the image of the Virgin of Guadelupe there on the wall. My healing comes from her. She came to me in a dream when I was still quite young, ordering me to become a *curandera*. So it is to her that the money is given. All my work is done through her. Otherwise, nothing permanent could be accomplished."

Another sickness familiar to the *curanderos* of the United States is *castigo de Dios,* a punishment from God. Occasionally, the patient is aware of the diagnosis before he seeks out the healer. One Mexican-American teenager sneaked into the home of a *curandero* when no one was looking because he was terrified his family would discover the nature of his sin. John, as he insisted on calling himself, told the *curandero* he had been stealing money from his father to buy wine and marijuana for almost a year. Lately, his head felt mushy and his arms felt soft, as if the bones in his body were made of foam rubber. He and a friend shared a motorbike, but he had had three accidents on the motorbike in the last month and his friend did not want him to use it any more. He was angry with his friend; but he knew in his heart the friend was right. His arms and legs were getting worse and worse. On his way to the *curandero*'s office, he had felt himself staggering like one drunk—and he had had nothing since yesterday.

The *curandero* launched into a course of treatment that lasted many months. On that first visit, he gave

John an egg massage accompanied by prayers. However, he cautioned the boy that the treatment would give him only temporary relief. "As long as God is angry with you, so long will you suffer. The only true cure can come when you have set yourself right in God's eyes."

After studying John for a long time in silence, the *curandero* told the boy that his instinct to keep his sin from his family was sound. His father would be too angry, and telling him would do him a great harm. He instructed John to make a full confession of his sins to God and, as a penance for his theft, to give his mother a sum of money each week. The boy promised to repay the amount of money he had stolen.

"No," the *curandero* said sternly. "You will give money until I tell you to stop. And I will not tell you to stop until you are married and have a son of your own."

The *curandero* admits he had previous knowledge of the family. It is not trickery, he says, but part of being a *curandero*. "I must know many things. I must give everything I know to the people who come to me. Juan is a good boy. It is his father who is the cause of the trouble. Juan's father is a great burden. He gambles everything. The money his wife makes as a day worker, he uses this way. The family do not eat well. There is little clothing. The furnishings of their house are of the kind that give the family shame before their friends. Evil begets evil. Juan's father sins against God when he shows no respect for the marriage that God blessed. The boy has been caught up in the evil. That is why he showed disrespect to his father. But this is wrong, too. The father's sins are his own. It is Juan's duty to respect his parents."

The *curandero* insisted that Juan come to his office

in secret every day for an egg massage and prayers. During each visit, he extracted from him a detailed account of his efforts to find a job so that he could begin his penance. Three weeks went by before Juan was able to find a job, and then it was a low-paying job washing dishes in a drugstore cafeteria. During this period, the *curandero* was sympathetic but firm in his insistence that the boy must find work or his symptoms would return with redoubled fury. He would not accept payment until after the boy had made his first payment to his mother.

Juan's symptoms did recur from time to time until he had made the tenth payment to his mother. At that time, the *curandero* told Juan that he had received a vision from Juan's patron saint, saying that God was now convinced Juan's intentions were sincere and the punishment had been removed.

The *curandero* was asked why he had not forbidden the boy to smoke marijuana. He shrugged. "Juan needed a job. The marijuana was a little thing. The boy smokes but little now. It was the way he felt toward his father that was important. Further, it is not wise to forbid what will not be obeyed."

Asked whether he had received his plan of treatment in a vision, he replied, "When I was young, the visions did not come easily. It took much preparation. Much concentration. Many prayers. Then, perhaps, the vision would come. Now, the vision is always there. As I talk to the patient, God puts into my head what to do."

In this country, it would not occur to a *curandero* that he was related to a *brujo*. The *brujo* is a servant of the Devil; a *curandero* belongs to God. However, both the *curandero*'s magic and the *brujo*'s are a heritage from the long-dead culture of the Aztecs.

CHAPTER NINE

El Brujo

Penetrating the invisible curtain that separates witches and their magic from non-witches is almost impossible. It is ironic that the oldest profession in the world is also the least known. Today, those who are sincerely interested in finding out about the craft cannot even discover who the witches are, much less what being a witch means.

Discussions of witches as seen from the outside are plentiful enough, and by comparing notes we can obtain a fairly complete picture of the way witches present themselves to the non-witch. Reassuringly, the results have not been a thick portfolio of radically differing views, but a composite portrait that cuts across time and space.

However, the portrait is the work of strangers. Descriptions from the witches' own mouths are limited and far from satisfactory in terms of interpretation. Our main source is the confessions wrung from the tortured victims of the church's four-century war against witches. Often, real understanding of this material is made difficult by the amount of time separating us from the event, the hostility and ignorance of the interrogators, confusion resulting from changes in language and culture, and the fact that the witches were naturally hostile witnesses.

Our only other familiar source, the occasional kook who announces publicly that he is a witch and will reveal the secrets of his calling, is about as convincing as a New York cowboy.

Witches claim their silence is not perverse. They say that, as some pigments cannot survive sunlight, so magic is destroyed by non-functional revelation.

Apparently, the witch's motives are the key factor. Respect for the craft is crucial to the calling. Unless the possessor of supernatural powers treats them with dignity, cherishes them, and protects them, he will lose his ability. It is as if his powers, or perhaps the spirits who supply them, become angry and move away.

In countries affected by Western civilization, the difficulty of discovering witches is greater than elsewhere. Centuries of disbelief, scorn, and hatred have made the inheritors of such witchcraft as has survived extremely wary.

In 1960, an event occurred whose probability is impossible to compute. The event has incalculable value to those seeking to penetrate the invisible curtain. A young man was befriended and accepted as a novice by a practicing *brujo*. Apprenticeship is the means by which witches perpetuate themselves. This in itself was not extraordinary. The stroke of luck was that the young man, a graduate student at one of the largest universities in the United States, was as preconditioned to publication as a witch is to secrecy.

The novice, Carlos Castaneda, spent a number of years struggling to enter the supernatural world that for his teacher had more reality than the supermarkets and concrete highways that abounded in the region where the two first met. In the end, Mr. Castaneda's American environment won out. He became unwilling to give up his identity and the system of beliefs he had lived by, beliefs that were threatened by the experiences of his apprenticeship. Nevertheless, by the time he withdrew from his training he had participated in adventures few people ever encounter.

In 1968, he wrote a book about his experiences as a witch's disciple titled *Don Juan: A Yaqui Way of Knowledge*. Anyone who has even a casual interest in witchcraft should make the book part of his library. It is available in paperback form on the newsstands, or it can be acquired by writing the publishers, Ballantine Books, Inc., 101 Fifth Avenue, New York, N.Y., 10003.

The publication of the book represents the triumph of this country's public school system over Mr. Castaneda's shorter-termed apprenticeship. Nevertheless, the affection and respect he felt for his teacher is clear throughout the book. And it is interesting that, even while he turns a spotlight on knowledge which has been kept hidden for centuries, Mr. Castaneda refuses to reveal certain points of information.

Perhaps the most tantalizing aspect of this glimpse of witchcraft is its confirmation of all the previous claims made about the craft. The teacher, don Juan, spoke matter-of-factly to his disciples of powers that most of us have experienced only in fantasy. Shape-changing was a skill don Juan spent considerable time trying to develop in his pupil. He explained that the original choice of animal is an individual matter, but once the selection has been made and the training period completed, the animal shape is fixed. No substitute form can be used. Don Juan himself had chosen to become a crow and found this bird so satisfactory as a secondary identity that he urged it on his disciple. As a crow, he could fly across the treetops on silent pinions. He also had the ability to transport himself through space without assuming his crow shape.

From the beginning, there was no doubt in Mr. Castaneda's mind about the effectiveness of don Juan's teaching methods. That, in fact, was the crux of the problem. The ease with which his teacher had him participating in supernatural activities increasingly frightened him.

Surprise was an important element in don Juan's methods. Often the lesson was completed before Castaneda knew what the day's subject was to be. On one occasion, when don Juan was trying to teach him to transport himself through space, he suddenly found himself alone and naked some distance from his teacher's house. The results of his exercises in reading minds, travelling into the past and future, and protecting himself from hostile sorcery were equally startling.

Don Juan made it clear that there were further abilities to be developed in his pupil when the time was ripe. He talked to the young man of the superhuman strength he had developed when he himself was a young man, and of the various occult methods of taking human life. He hinted at other abilities which he could not yet reveal. However, at all times don Juan emphasized that although a witch's powers were far-reaching and important, the wisdom to be gained through sorcery was more significant and more satisfying.

One of the most enlightening aspects of the book is the opportunity it presents to see don Juan's attitude toward himself and his profession. He never spoke of himself as a *curandero*, a healing witch. He was a *brujo*, and his pride in his calling was great. He was frank, even offhand about acknowledging his capacity to murder and injure. However, it is obvious from the conversations Mr. Castaneda reports that don Juan did not think of himself as evil. He was aware that he had been given the opportunity to develop vast power as a doer of evil. But it was not his nature to behave in this way. He preferred wisdom to power over men. It is equally obvious that Mr. Castaneda shares his teacher's assessment of his character. After reading the book, few will feel like arguing with their conclusions.

Don Juan emerges from Mr. Castaneda's memory as a man of great wisdom. There are hints of ethics that are not those taught in our public school system. However, it could be argued that the differences between Juan's individualism and the public social conscience of this country is merely one of words. Our society pretends to a tender-heartedness that is not often apparent in its behavior. In the matter of morality, don Juan emerges superior to most of us. Here is a man who had grasped great power and could have reached out his hand and taken more. Instead, he withdrew from it because it made him uncomfortable. He preferred wisdom to power. And he desired wisdom not for the sense of superiority it gave him but for itself.

One of don Juan's most prominent characteristics was his sense of responsibility. His gratitude and affection for his own teacher, his "benefactor" as he called him, had not weakened with time. He responded to that debt by continually studying the lessons he had been given, determined that nothing his teacher had taught him should be wasted. At the same time, he recognized that he and his teacher were two distinct personalities with strongly differing inclinations. He was able to see that certain paths his benefactor took would be wrong for him and to go his own way resolutely but with unwavering respect. He brought the same attitudes to sorcery. He exploited the supernatural world, but always with reverence for the spirits that befriended and guided him, and he would not allow his student to do less. With the spirits, as with his benefactor, he discriminated between those that were compatible with his nature and the life he wanted and those that were not; the latter he avoided, although recognizing the vast powers they could give him.

With his disciple he was tender, solicitous, firm, or demanding as the occasion required. Obviously, he had planned to give over a considerable chunk of his life to training his disciple. Obligation and gratitude were not in his eyes the purpose of the gift. He wanted to help his disciple to become a witch. The completion of that goal would be his reward.

As an individualist, he respected the individuality of others. His hope that his disciple would choose the path of wisdom rather than the path of power was patent. However, he had already accepted the possibility that his student's character might not allow such a decision.

One gets the impression that don Juan's benefactor claimed his prerogatives in the classic tradition of the *brujo*. The benefactor controlled and manipulated lesser persons, terrorized and injured his enemies, and casually amused himself with occult pyrotechnics regardless of the distress of others.

Nevertheless, even though don Juan referred to his teacher as a *diablero*—literally, a devilist—there is no suggestion that he thought his teacher was an agent of Satan. Don Juan seemed singularly unconcerned with formal religion. His attention was directed toward the spirit world, which was at once the source of his power and the university in which he was enrolled. His attitude toward God seems to be akin to the Aztec attitude toward Ometecuhtli: acknowledgment but lack of interaction.

He was not concerned with the subtleties of reality. For him, nature existed on a continuum, and the point at which what we call natural drifts into what we call supernatural did not interest him. Again and again, his disciple tried to question him on this point. Each time, don Juan reacted with bewilderment and impatience. The discussion was meaningless to him, and he felt it distracted his pupil's attention from the things he should be learning.

The beings with whom he was involved he spoke of as allies and teachers. These beings were the power essences of three hallucinogenic plants, each of which is familiar by reputation to Westerners. According to don Juan, access to the abilities of a *brujo* comes only through the acceptance of the apprentice by these power essences. It was necessary to proceed with caution and approach each of these beings in precisely the correct fashion. Don Juan's sponsorship was no guarantee that these beings would accept his disciple. All the *brujo* could do was arrange the introduction: then the pupil was on his own. If any one of the beings should indicate the slightest annoyance with the stranger, don Juan advised immediate withdrawal and was emphatic about the recklessness of a second attempt.

To ensure the greatest possibility of acceptance, don Juan stressed the importance of strict attention to details of procedure. The impression is that any deviation from the prescribed ritual would be interpreted by the being as an affront to its dignity. Again and again don Juan made the point that these beings were dangerous unless approached properly. More than mere personalities, these beings were power sources. Carelessness in their presence could be as fatal as carelessness with electricity, atomic radiation, or sunshine.

Nevertheless, these beings were distinguished by definite, unique personalities. It would be impossible to confuse one with another. In the beginning, Mr. Castaneda had trouble accepting his teacher's views on this subject. It is difficult for someone brought up in a Western culture to think of a cactus—or the power essence within the cactus—as having a personality of its own. Not don Juan, but his own experiences finally convinced him.

The power source residing in the peyote cactus don Juan referred to as Mescalito. In time, Mr. Castaneda saw Mescalito for himself. The form was hominoid, not necessarily human but strongly masculine in character. However, don Juan said that Mescalito appears to different people in different shapes. The shape is insignificant, it is the relationship that is important. Once Mescalito has accepted a person, he keeps the same shape when he is with him.

Don Juan was anxious for his disciple to be accepted by Mescalito, because he felt this being would be able to instruct and protect him on levels that were not accessible to humans, even if they were *brujos*. Mr. Castaneda approached the interview in mixed disbelief and bewilderment. The experience was disturbing to him because it turned his view of the world around him topsey-turvey. He began to understand the significance of his experience when he saw don Juan's relief that he had come through the meeting safely.

The incident caused him to approach the other drugs

with more caution and apprehension. However, his teacher urged him to proceed despite the danger, pointing out that although the risks were great they were necessary for the achievement of his goal.

Next, don Juan arranged for a confrontation with the *yerba del diablo*—devil's weed, or as it is called north of the border, Jimson weed. Jimson weed can be as deadly as its lily-like flowers are beautiful. Don Juan claimed that the plant had the fickle-minded, capricious personality of a flirtatious woman. Properly tamed, the plant yields the powers one associates with the name *brujo*. Like many seductive women, the plant will destroy a man's character if he is not strong. And if the plant takes a dislike to a person, it delights in making him suffer.

Don Juan told his pupil that the *yerba del diablo* had not liked him when he had tried it as a novice and had, in fact, almost succeeded in killing him. Despite his own experience, he urged his disciple to attempt a friendship with the plant because of the opportunities the relationship would provide.

To Mr. Castaneda's surprise and consternation, the plant showed promise of responding affectionately toward him. His association with it was dramatic and took place by slow, careful degrees that made him more apprehensive with each success. Before he terminated his apprenticeship, the plant had already given him a taste of the strength and awesome power of divination it offered its favorites.

The use of the hallucinogenic mushroom was the most hazardous of the three undertakings. Don Juan cautioned his disciple that a single mistake could result in the death of either or both of them. The personality of the drug did not reside in the mushroom proper, but in the smoke—*humito*, don Juan called it—which was produced by smoking a pipeful of a carefully prepared mixture of herbs including the mushroom. Properly done, the ingredients for the mixture can be gathered, dried, and shredded only once a year and must be consumed or destroyed by the conclusion of a twelve-month period. Each step in preparing the mixture is crucial. Selecting the mushroom from among myriads of its close relatives is perhaps the most critical stage, since at least one of its favorite companions is deadly.

The treatment of the pipe in which the mixture is to be smoked is gravely important. The pipe is not an unfeeling, insentient object. It must be approached and wooed. Don Juan gave Mr. Castaneda his own pipe, saying that it would not be safe to approach *humito* in any other way. The act was by no means as simple as handing him the pipe. First, don Juan allowed his disciple to see the pipe. This was the first time since it had been in his possession that don Juan had exposed it to another's gaze. Months later, Castaneda was permitted to touch it. Later still, he was given the opportunity of handling the pipe. Each step of this process was filled with anxiety for student and teacher alike. At no point was the end certain. But despite the hazards to them both, don Juan urged his pupil forward, for among the powers *humito* could grant was that of shape-changing.

In the face of these marvels, don Juan was definite in emphasizing the limitations of a witch's power. He knew of no way to master old age, for one. He spoke of old age as an enemy, the cruelest of all. It was possible to engage in a running battle with old age and keep it at a distance for a long time, but the battle lasted only as long as the witch's courage. The moment he gave in to fatigue and pain, old age took over and left him a foolish, powerless old man.

Another enemy against which he was helpless was social change. The times are out of joint for sorcery, and the times were like an ocean breaking over don Juan's identity as a witch and slowly eroding it. Once, he had used his craft regularly and with zest. Since then, he has come to lose interest in these powers. Not only he, but all *brujos* are withdrawing from occult practices, because the environment is hostile to them. White men, he said, refused to credit the evidence of their senses. Indians knew what they saw, but the seeing terrified them. He suggested that to be purposeful for others and satisfying to the witch, sorcery must be practiced in a world oriented to its use.

Unlike that of Jívaro witches, don Juan's gradual retirement was voluntary and not in the least dangerous to him. Both disciplines require the use of hallucinogenics as the first necessary step in sorcery. However, the drugs used are different, and it may be that their differing natures account for the difference in the duration of the supernatural powers one obtains from them. Another factor may be equally if not more important. Don Juan discovered that once his friendship with the essences of the power-sources was on a firm foundation, he no longer required their chemical properties to enter the supernatural world. He could become a crow whether he smoked the mushroom mixture or not. He was able to consult with Mescalito without chewing peyote buttons.

As don Juan repeated so frequently, the power sources are dangerous. Perhaps one of the dangers is overexposure to their chemical properties.

CHAPTER TEN

Vestigial Witchcraft and New Growth

The old religion, as witches call it, survives in the nooks and crannies of Europe like an ancient pine growing out of a crack in a sheer rock cliff. The tree is dwarfed from lack of nourishment. The wind has twisted and bent its limbs. The wonder is that it has managed to stay alive. It has its own grotesque beauty: the reflection of the indomitable life force.

In Europe, a tourist has little hope of picking out those who secretly practice witchcraft. When a stranger comes to a small rural village and starts poking around and asking questions, he receives no answers. Prodding results in hostility and lies, or in stubborn silence. Only a man or woman, or preferably a married couple, who stays in a village long enough to be thought of as a resident has a chance at the information. Even then, direct questioning plugs the communication channels.

However, if the interest and concern for the people of the village is real, if the mind is alert to a chance remark, a veiled allusion, an overheard comment, little by little a picture of the real thing can be constructed.

The sorcerer himself will probably remain elusive, or at least withdrawn. Centuries of suspicion have taken their toll, and a kind of functional paranoia has been handed down from parent to child. Consequently, this record of vestigial witchcraft in Europe is really a grab bag of incidents that were chanced upon by good luck or, to the horror of the principals, were discovered by the press.

In Lueneburg, West Germany, the tragic story of a young boy who was beaten to death by his own father uncovered an entire region in which medieval witchcraft was still alive. The father had been attempting to help his son by ridding his body of the devil that had taken possession of him; however, the body turned out not to be as strong as the devil's grip. Reporters' curiosity was aroused by the father's story, and they began investigating the countryside between the Elbe and Weser Rivers in lower Saxony. The evidence they collected eventually forced the West German Ministry of Social Affairs to make its own investigation.

It was a district little affected by the industrial revolution. The traditions of the blighting witch and the curing witch had been handed down from parent to child, generation after generation. After the depression that brought the Nazis to power, witchcraft all but disappeared in the enthusiasm for the new Germany. Science and progress aroused the peasants' expectations of a new life of prosperity and happiness. But when Hitler and the new Germany led only to ruined houses, bomb-scarred fields, death, hunger, disease, and twisted bodies, the people of lower Saxony returned to the old ways.

They returned with a vengeance.

More than half the population still shuns medical doctors, putting faith in supernatural healing. Before the deluge of notoriety, the old remedies were openly used and openly sold. Most of the potions are purchased directly from the *Teufelsdienerin*, literally the servant of the devil; that is to say, witch. Some of the simpler ones can be prepared at home, if one has the courage to obtain the ingredients.

A cure for lumbago is a drink made from seven beetles that have died of hunger, pulverized in a mortar that also contains six laurel berries and then stirred into water until the particles are suspended.

To ensure that a child's teeth will grow in straight without sore gums, pull a tooth from the mouth of a live mouse. Drill a hole through the mouse's tooth, hang it from a ribbon or chain, and have the child wear it around his neck. This remedy will also help adults who have a toothache.

To cool a raging fever requires a magical knife and cannot be accomplished by a non-professional. The *Teufelsdienerin* catches a black cat. Cutting the cat's left ear with her witch's knife, she holds the cat so that its blood drops on a piece of black bread. Then she has her patient eat the bread.

The chief ingredient of the potion for ridding oneself of warts is easier to come by in Germany, with its many old abandoned graveyards, than it would be in this country. A circle of human skull is required about an inch in diameter. If the wart is growing on a man, a man's skull must be used; if on a woman, a woman's skull. The bone is heated over the coals of a wood fire until drops of sweat appear on its surface. The sweat is then wiped off with the cutting edge of a knife. The sweat is boiled until it dries into a fine powder, which is stirred into hot ale and drunk before it has a chance to cool.

The remedy for alcoholism is disagreeable to prepare. The first step is to catch a toad; a frog will not do. While the toad is still alive, the *Teufelsdienerin* must tear it in two. The pieces are cooked over a log fire in a ceramic urn until they have been charred to ash. The ashes are mixed with brandy and must be drunk in a single gulp.

Many of the diseases besetting the countryside of lower Saxony are not susceptible to treatment by potion. These are the ailments that have been brought on by enchantment.

The German blighting witches, like those of Guatemala, having lost their legitimate function, have turned their hostile talents inward on their own communities. No one knows when one of the witches will strike next. For a sum of money, for a grudge, the witch applies her arts and the victim is struck down. The towns and farmlands seethe with fear and suspicion. Revenge hexing against those who are suspected of hiring a witch only tightens the spiral of hatred. Persons who have inherited anti-hex incantations and charms are kept busy undoing the mischief. Unfortunately, they have realized that theirs is a seller's market and have upped their prices beyond the reach of a good part of the community. A dehexing spell is going for as much as five hundred marks. That comes to more than a hundred dollars, a price that represents a lot of hard work for a farmer.

In a desperate effort to control the runaway terrorism by sorcery, actual arrests of the most irresponsible of the blighting witches have been made. Seventy of these cases have come to trial. But trials do not cure the bodies that are already suffering from the witch's curses, and fines and imprisonment do not put an end to malevolence. And further, for every witch brought before the law, three continue their free-wheeling tyranny without detection.

The farm people are becoming so panicky that the tension has caused acts of violence. Heinz Sammann killed his own grandfather with an ax on the suspicion, unconfirmed by evidence, that the old man had been hexing his cows. A farmer whose daughter showed the signs of wasting away as if from a hex stoned a neighbor lady he had been feuding with for years, under the mistaken assumption that she was responsible.

The government is slowly being forced to move in and forcibly put an end to the violence. Tragically, we may be sure it will be done in such a way as to put an end to witchcraft as well. There will be a clamor for "proper" education to do away with superstition. Teams of educators will move into the Lower Saxony area and begin a long-term process of "enlightening" the children. They will be taught that magic is nonsense, that only psychotics think they are witches, that hexsickness is a psychosomatic disturbance of the neurotic individual. Eventually, they will know better than to believe in their own wild talents, and one of the last remnants of ancient powers will disappear.

In Italy one observer, a shrewd young woman, was able to pinpoint a center of magical practices when she noticed that none of her Italian friends ever spoke of a certain village by name. Whenever they had occasion to refer to it, they used the phrase *Quel Paese,* which means That Town.

The discovery touched off a long, slow, carefully-executed stint of detective work on her part. She quickly discovered that direct questions produced only blank looks. Indirection took longer, but at least it got results. In time she found out that the town's name was not spoken because so much magic was practiced within its boundaries that the name itself had developed a power of its own. Uttering the town's name weakened the speaker. Even if it was said accidentally, even if the individual touched iron immediately after speaking the taboo name, the fact remained that if he should enter the town at some future date he would be quickly struck down by the evil eye.

Cynics often say that it is the beliefs of a superstitious person that make him susceptible to sickness from hexing or the evil eye. Our lady detective, however, discovered an instance in which the reverse was true. A friend of hers, an Italian surveyor, was a great skeptic about the supernatural. Nothing made him as angry as any display of belief. He would launch into long tirades on the fraud or foolishness involved in "magic." He was especially annoyed by the refusal of the villagers to name *Quel Paese*, and he took great delight in naming the town in front of them at every opportunity.

Eventually his business forced him to make the trip to *Quel Paese*. Everyone in the village knew of his habit of mentioning the town by name and mocking the power of its magic. Consequently, no one would accompany him to the town. If he wanted to call down the wrath of ancient magic on his head, that was his affair. The villagers did not want to be around when the consequences struck.

Raging at the villagers' credulity, the surveyor hired a mule. The ride was bumpy, dusty, and uneventful. Then he reached *Quel Paese*, and somewhere between its outposts and his destination in town, the mule bucked him off its back. The surveyor flew through the air and came down neatly skewered on a thick iron pike.

He was three months in the hospital and six months recovering. Eventually every part of him was restored to normal health—except his cynicism. That died in *Quel Paese*.

In Italy, the evil eye is referred to as "overlooking." It is common there. Nursing mothers are taught to be alert to a malign glance that may dry up their flowing milk; at its touch, they will quickly recite a counterspell they have memorized against the need.

Mussolini's son-in-law, Count Ciano, was said to be a skilled overlooker. There were those who suggested it was due more to his talents than to his father-in-law's political adroitness that Mussolini was able to take over Italy. The dictator's death and the contemptuous way in which his body and Count Ciano's were hung by the heels following Italy's surrender toward the end of World War II in no way diminished public confidence in either hexing or the evil eye. By that time, both men had had a goodly share of both directed at them by heartbroken parents who had lost their sons in a senseless war.

None of the lady detective's stratagems succeeded in wangling an introduction to the most powerful witch in *Quel Paese* or her daughter. There was no point in meeting the witch, she was told, because she had grown old and never practiced her craft these days. Yes, she had a daughter, but the daughter was not a witch. Besides, no one believed in that sort of thing anymore. That was for old people.

In a fleeting moment of carelessness, one woman admitted that the daughter could occasionally be persuaded to help someone as a favor. But not even as a favor would the daughter meet the lady detective. Or it may be that they met and talked every day of her visit and she never knew who she was.

Poverty forced a local charm-maker to be less distant. Once, the charm-maker, incensed at a false rendering of a charm that had been printed in a book, actually forgot herself so far as to chant the charm in its true form. As the verses progressed, her voice altered from its normal contralto to a nasal singsong that was scarcely recognizable. Her eyes glazed and she seemed lost within herself as the ancient formula that shields an infant against disease slowly spilled from her lips.

For the most part, however, the woman refused to discuss her talent and how she had come by it, although she did indicate that her powers were inherited rather than learned. Another fascinating detail was that her powers seemed to increase during her menstrual flow. Usually, in *Quel Paese,* a woman was considered to be off her game, so to speak, at that time. Strenuous or delicate tasks were put off until the next week. But at that time, the charm-maker was considered especially adept in everything she did. The town women would approach her then and ask her to do some task for them. It was as if she personified the Earth Mother Goddess at that time and blessed whatever she touched.

Spain also has a race of witches. They are segregated, exploited, and hunted down as the mood strikes the Spaniards. They are the gypsies, of course; and it is difficult to decide whether they are discriminated against because of their race or their sorcery. Some of the old folk magic is still remembered and practiced in the provinces by the Spanish peasants, but the sophisticated magic is in the hands of the gypsies. They grub for the herbs, roots, and seeds. They brew and sell the potions. They tell fortunes by palmistry, reading the cards, or scrying.

It would be a mistake to imagine the gypsies as a gentle folk who never give tit for tat. Their poisons are feared more than guns. And the only thing dreaded more than gypsy poison is a gypsy curse.

They are also adept at curing, and this presents the Spaniards with a dilemma; for a gypsy cure may also contain a gypsy curse. For this reason, the Spaniards try to attend to their own health needs, combining the use of centuries-old recipes and prayers to appropriate saints with the buying of candles and the paid singing of a mass. It is only when an illness refuses to respond to such treatment that the family goes to the gypsies for help. The price for a cure runs high. Worse, they can never feel quite certain that the cure is untainted.

The quarrel between the two cultures is as old as their coexistence in the same living space. The Spaniards claim the gypsies are thieves, kidnappers, and murderers. The gypsies claim nothing. They shrug and spit on the ground when the Spanish are mentioned.

The Spanish charges are true. It is also true that the Spaniards use the gypsies for whipping-boys, hunting them down whenever they feel depressed or anxious and covering their sport with a legal excuse. In recent years, Franco's internal policies have done nothing to help calm the passions of the two groups.

With this background it is easy to understand why the gypsies are delighted to be hired to curse a Spaniard. The leader of one band, whom a few weeks of shared food and wine had made friendly, laughed when it was suggested he enjoyed this type of work. "I am very careful with the spells," he said. "And I charge little. These Spanish are a stingy lot. If I charged what

I was worth, they would hesitate so long over parting with the pesos, they would recover from their ill humor."

Since love potions almost invariably lead to cuckolded husbands and despoiled virgins in the peculiar Spanish approach to sex, gypsies are well pleased to keep those prices down as well, and generally manage to do a brisk trade fostering the love business.

The gypsies say their small numbers prevent them from winning the long struggle, but that the Spaniards lose even when they win. The leader of the band declared, "In our own way we will fight them to a standstill. We are more valuable to them than they realize. One day they will leave us alone, then . . . Who knows?" He shrugged, but he could not bring himself to say they would be friends.

Charms to calm the sea and to keep away its monsters are common among the Portuguese fishermen. In the long months the men are fighting the sea, their women wonder if they will ever see them again and perform ceremonies that did not originate in Rome. However, in Portugal the church has been wise. The priest officiates at some of these ceremonies and ignores others. All Portuguese magic is church-oriented, and the people think of themselves as Catholics, not as witches.

With the Basques it is different; or at least, so the stories go. Although they are a jovial, friendly people, they have a genius for keeping personal matters to themselves. Franco's soldiers, whom the Basques do not love, swear that the mountain people are not Christians at all and that the village churches are nothing more than a pretense. It is hard to judge the truth of these stories because feeling runs high on both sides of the invisible line in the Basque villages. And the soldiers stationed there to keep the people in line are peculiarly accident-prone.

For what it is worth, the soldiers tell of half-empty churches whose seats are used only by women-folk. The men slip off to the mountains, where they disappear into rock caves to practice another religion. From recesses dug in the walls, the ancient animal masks and skin robes are pulled out, the headdresses of antlers, the immense, carved phalluses of horn. And from the mouths of the caves come the muffled sound of drumbeats and chanting. The soldiers insist that the pagan rites carried out in these caves include human sacrifice and cannibalism. They have had comrades-in-arms who went into the mountains and never came out again, and whose bodies were never found. Those men, the soldiers bitterly assert, ended their military careers as offerings to an unknown god.

In France, there is no question that the old religion is being practiced. Not the pre-Christian heritage of the Basques, this witchcraft is a derivative of late Renaissance satanism.

French neo-satanism is an urban rather than a rural development, taken up by a part of the artistic-intellectual set, the spiritual grandchildren of the rebels who had been bohemians in the twenties and communists in the thirties. The neo-satanists are mostly young people who have given up politics in despair of achieving constructive programs in the dizzy whirlpool of French politics and in many cases have given up art, too, except on a decadent, backbiting, purely verbal level. Their creative energies are spent on the improbable masked ball of the Black Mass. They take the specifics of their pageantry from moldy books rather than their parents' memories. Still, their fervor, their hatred of the world around them, and their avid attention to detail gives these witch gatherings a chilling authenticity.

Drug-taking is expected, the choice of drugs is wide, and a sense of caution about the practice is nonexistent. Partly, this results from the fact that contemporary transportation makes a global drug trade possible. The drugs are in Paris, but not the people who use them ceremonially and respect their power.

The result is chaos. At one Black Mass held on the night of December twenty-fourth, circulating among the mob of over two hundred celebrants were hashish, cocaine, laudanum, LSD, peyote, sleeping pills of various kinds and strengths, Jimson weed, belladonna berries, many types of amphetamines, methadrine, synthetic mescaline, and metal tanks of sodium pentothal and carbon dioxide, complete with breathing apparatus.

By four in the morning, the scene could have been mistaken for a film version of Dante's *Inferno*. Costumes and masks were strewn over the floor. The different rock bands were blasting away, the musicians oblivious not only to the other group but to each other. Around the edges of the bands there was frenzied dancing. Sexual athletics had taken over the area in which the mass had been celebrated. Twenty or more of the drug-takers were rolling around the floor, writhing and screaming in simulated or real terror of their visions. No one was attempting to soothe them, because the worse their trip, the more successful they were in terms of group mores. Next day, the drug-takers would compare notes and argue about which of them had "gone farthest into hell." It was said that the competition was intense.

The guide and interpreter of the sabbat was a ceramist who was not himself a satanist but made a point of attending as many sabbats as possible because they provided him with such rich visual experiences. "I've used the images for a number of large frescos," he said. "I call them 'Nightmares.'"

It was suggested that one day a drugged witch would not be able to climb up out of hell under her own power and would require medical assistance. The ceramist grinned. "It has already happened. More than once. And there have been suicides. Some quite spectacular. To date the coven has been kept out of it. As far as the police know, and the press, these were isolated events. One day someone will talk. Then all hell will break loose. Scandal. Police raids. Notoriety. Perhaps some more suicides. The coven will fall apart. Soon a new one will start up. I have seen the cycle many times."

When asked whether any of these witches had been successful in obtaining magical powers, he laughed. "Magic! There is no magic here. Here there is anarchy. Anger. Disbelief. Here there is masquerade. But no magic. For magic you must have belief. I come from Normandy, from the wild coast country, and I know. . . ."

He trailed off, pursing his lips. He was asked what he knew. He responded with a shake of the head. "I know magic is dead," he said lamely. "There are no more real witches."

He was asked what he knew of the old days when witches had lived. The question made him more evasive. "Our grandmothers told us stories. Perhaps that's all they were: stories."

That witchcraft is practiced behind the Iron Curtain is an intriguing possibility. Rumors claim it is more than a possibility. Officially, the communist countries are anti-religion. Functionally, however, rumors claim that in Hungary, Poland, and Czechoslovakia the old knowledge of enchantments and poisons are used in attempts to drive the Russians beyond the national borders.

If this rumor is true, it would suggest that in recent years Russia may have turned a dour face to her own witches, assuming they exist. If they do, they would be a most interesting group to study. In the time of Catherine the Great, the reputation of Russian witches had reached as far west as France. This is hardly surprising, since old Russia was a rich melting-pot of different kinds of witchcraft. Within her eastern borders the warrior magic of the Mongols lingered. Cabbalah, the sorcery of the Jews, came to Russia with that population and survived the pograms. Her Eskimo population in Siberia claims that its survival in the snow deserts can be directly attributed to prowess in sorcery. And in the heartland of old Russia, the fertility religions never completely yielded to Christianity.

When the revolution changed Russian life, witchcraft was very much a part of the culture. Almost every Russian peasant was at least a part-time witch. There is no saying how many communist witches exist today. Propaganda from the state educational system directed against any kind of mysticism has been intense and persistent. The question remains: has it been effective?

England, long the symbol of conservative conventionality, has suddenly taken up witchcraft with spectacular zest. Strangely enough, the traditionally stodgy middle class, and especially its middle-aged members, are in the forefront of the movement. The reason for the sudden enthusiasm may be that this group has explored materialism to its last nook and cranny and has found it sadly wanting. They have tried self-improvement, private and state education, and nationalized socialism. It is not that they do not appreciate what the state does for them; but they have come to realize there are some things the state cannot do for them. They are presently engaged in improving their metaphysical lives.

Covens are popping up like mushrooms throughout the British Isles. With their usual thoroughness, the English are exploring witchcraft both by doing library research and by searching out those who have inherited knowledge. It is a witch hunt of a different flavor. The atmosphere of the new English witchcraft is healthier and more exciting than that across the Channel. In England, the covens are in communication with each other. Almost every issue of *Fate*, an English magazine devoted to metaphysics, carries news of the formation of a fledgling group. In this way, the novice witches learn from each other's successes and mistakes.

In 1965, one of the most firmly established of the new covens revived an ancient ceremony in Chipping Norton with the celebration of a sabbat. The witches came together to dance around a bonfire in the full of the moon and chant a cry heard on that island before the English language itself was born: *Eko Eko Azarak, Eko Eko Zomelak, Eko Eko Gananas, Eko Eko Arada.*

This particular coven, like so many of the new English covens, reaches back to the true beginnings of witchcraft in their attempt to revive the fertility religions of antiquity. The practice of magic is combined with the worship of the sun god and the moon goddess. All the rituals of the coven have the purpose of bringing man and nature back into a harmonious, working relationship. In part this is accomplished, as it has always been accomplished in fertility religions, by symbolically emphasizing man's responsibility to nature. Man cannot afford to be only a taker in the relationship; he must be a giver, too. In the Chipping Norton ceremony, the witches acknowledged life's debt to the sun by dancing in a circle around a bonfire and leaping over its flames to strengthen the sun god in his annual struggle against chaos and cold.

Eleanor Bone, the articulate high priestess of this coven, admits that it will be many a day before her coven will be accepted by society as a legitimate religious entity. Until then, she and the rest of the coven try to endure with good grace the bad jokes and raw curiosity. The worst problem is that the rites of this coven are performed in the nude. The disrobing has a serious metaphysical purpose, as do all the minutiae of the rituals. They have discovered that the power of their collective blessing ceremonies and other occult practices is vitiated by clothes.

Nudity has become the rule. However, it is a rule that has created serious organizational problems. The high priestess has had to take pains in weeding out those who want to join the coven in the hopes it will be a cross between a nudity club and a group of swingers. The problem is aggravated by the coven's size, which is considerably larger than the late medieval thirteen and suggests the original concept of a congregation of worshippers. Naturally, the larger its numbers, the less control there is over group activity and the greater the likelihood that one fraudulent member will bring the entire group into disrepute. Thanks to Mrs. Bone's intuition, which at times seems suspiciously close to second sight, her coven has been spared such a disaster.

Although within the coven the emphasis on the craft and pride in being witches is strong, outwardly it stresses the religious theme in order to reduce the curiosity of reporters. The word *witch* comes from the Anglo-Saxon meaning "wise one," but to most of their contemporaries it implies All Hallows' Eve, black cats, caldrons, peaked hats, and warts on the nose.

Eleanor Bone, a handsome woman, doesn't own a peaked hat or a wart, but she does have a caldron. It is an essential tool of her craft. There are others. The altar is the first, and it is carefully aligned east and west. Candles light it, each colored to suggest symbolically the purpose of the sabbat. On the altar sits a silver chalice. Near the chalice lies a hazelwood wand. The wand's shape represents the phallus, which is infused with the power of fire. The hazel tree has mystical associations as powerful as those of oak; the wood itself is believed to have innate power. Folk tales say that faery wands were made of hazelwood; and even today, throughout Europe and America many dowsers use divining rods cut from hazel trees. The caldron—it is small enough to hold in the palm of one hand—holds water, a symbol of the Earth Mother Goddess.

Scented smoke rises from the censer, an offering to the goddess. Near the censer stands a pentacle, a flat piece of metal on which symbols of the earth have been engraved. A length of rope representing the spiritual union of the members of the coven is folded near the pentacle. The scourge lying nearby, a symbol of purification, has a functional purpose in certain ceremonies. Purification is symbolized by a bowl of salt as well. The last tool on the altar is a specially-made, black-handled knife, representing the element air and called by the witches an *athamé*.

Only the *athamé* can be used to trace the magic circle that is essential to all of the ceremonies. When the London fog forces the coven inside to do their dancing and chanting under an apartment roof rather than the sky, after the *athamé* has marked off the nine-foot circle, a bit of charcoal or chalk is used to make the pattern discernible to humans as well as spirits.

The *athamé* has other functions. Many recipes for

potions require that one or more of the ingredients be cut by an *athamé*. This is especially true of substances that are thought to be inhabited by spirits, who would consider it disrespectful to cut their dwelling places with an ordinary knife. For this reason each novice witch, upon entering a coven, has an *athamé* made for her use alone.

The English covens meet once a month in meetings they call esbats, rather than holding the traditional weekly meeting. The pressures of urban living make more frequent contact impossible. As it is, many of the members have trouble attending the esbats regularly.

In addition to these, there are four minor sabbats and four critical ones. The minor sabbats celebrate the seasons. The spring equinox comes on March twenty-first. The summer solstice, the longest day of the year, is June twenty-first, and the autumn equinox is on September twenty-first. And the winter solstice, celebrated with the Yule ceremony, is the shortest day of the year, December twenty-first.

The great sabbats are held to reinforce the breeding cycles of plants and animals. Candlemas, the ceremony of the lights, is far older than the church that put it to the use of commemorating the purification of the Virgin Mary. Held on February first, Candlemas emphasizes the rebirth of nature after winter's demise, shown in the green budding of spring.

May Eve, the sabbat called *Beltane*, is a fire festival in which the sun is strengthened as a life-giving principle by the worshippers who leap over the flames of their bonfire, as was done at Chipping Norton. The Gaelic word for the festival is *Bealltainn*. Today, unknowingly, many Scots and Irish in their churches join the witches in honoring May Eve. The festival is an important fertility ceremony for the coven. The witches, mounted on broomsticks symbolizing the phallus, leap high into the air. The higher they leap, the higher the crops will grow that summer.

Mrs. Bone insists that in her coven the other traditional fertility rite is symbolized by a token kiss representing the fructifying mating of humans. However, there was a time when the followers of the fertility religions stimulated the newly planted crops by performing ritualized sexual intercourse, often in the growing fields.

Lammas is a harvest celebration held on the first day of August. This festival is pure holiday; the year's work and worry is over, at least for a few days, and man rejoices and gives thanks for nature's bounty.

In *Samhain* (which translates as *Summer Ends*) or, as it is more commonly known, Halloween, the Beltane rites of leaping over a fire are repeated to strengthen the sun for the cold winter months ahead.

Anyone who has ever gone trick-or-treating associates broomsticks and peaked hats with witches. However, the custom that requires a coven to have both a high priest and a high priestess is less well known. A fertility religion naturally requires that both the male and the female principle be represented in the power structure. The high priest initiates female witches, the high priestess males.

The high priestess leads the coven's rites during the spring and summer months when the earth, the female principle, is awake. Beginning with the November sabbat of *Samhain*, the high priest takes over. Symbolizing the horned god of the underworld, he wears a headdress that looks rather like a Viking helmet. The sign of the horn holds dual powers: it represents both the crescent horns of the moon and the male element. The priest resides over the fall and winter ceremonies to symbolize the insertion of seeds into the earth to wait for the next spring awakening.

Next to the sabbats, the most important ceremony for the witches is that celebrating the adoption of new members. The novices are led naked to the sacred circle. There they are informed by the high priestess, if they are male, that it would be better to die than to come to the altar, unless they come with a joy that knows no fear, with perfect love and perfect trust.

Eleanor Bone's coven does not scourge the novices, but many of the new covens do. For this act of purification, the ritual whip that lies on the altar is used to strike the required number of blows on the novice's back. Following the purification, the novice is kissed five times by the priestess. Then he is introduced to the tools of his craft and consecrated with wine and oil. The celebration culminates in a feast of wine and cakes.

To advance to the level of a high priestess requires a second initiation. Again, there is purification by scourging. However, in keeping with the increased responsibility of the position, the number of blows is three times those given to the novice.

At the time of her second initiation, the priestess chooses her secret name and receives a red ribbon to be used as a garter. The garter has long been an identifying symbol of witches. Recent scholars have speculated that this may have been what Edward III of England was referring to when, in 1344, he picked up the fallen garter of a female courtier and exclaimed in a loud voice, "*Honi soit qui mal y pense*" (Evil come to him who evil thinks). There has even been speculation that the Order of the Garter founded by the king two years later, now the oldest and most important order of knighthood in England, was originally a royal coven.

In England, the serious purpose of the covens is viewed with good-natured amusement by non-witches. One scoffer, teasing an attractive nurse who had recently joined a coven, pointed out that actually little was known about the old fertility religions and that the ceremonies amounted to nothing more than dress-up games. "Or," he leered, "perhaps I should say dress-down games."

She looked him straight in the face. "I think it is better not to know and have a seeking spirit than to think you know everything and have a closed mind," she replied.

There is a great sense of exploration and investigation within the covens. How much is being accomplished in their occult studies is impossible for an outsider to determine because of their vow of secrecy.

"My God, it isn't that I don't *want* to tell you, old boy," one governmental employee said to a persistent inquirer. "But just suppose the old warnings were right. I'd lose the effect of three years of hard work. Besides, if the coven found out, I'd be ousted in a flash. They're quite firm about the vow business, don't you know."

The hard work to which he referred is the practice in concentration that all the new witches must undertake as part of their daily routine. The announced purpose of the practice is to gain the ability to scry, to read the future by interpreting the visions that form on a bright, smooth-surfaced object such as the Aztec's black obsidian mirror.

They may have other goals about which they do not care to be as frank. Snatches of conversation suggest that the caldron occasionally holds potions of belladonna and amanita. These two drugs are known to have been used by England's early witches to gain the power of teleportation.

One librarian, a recent graduate from Oxford who has been practicing on her own, was more voluble. "I put in a year trying to meditate, two, three hours a day, every day. At the end of my program, I was no further along than the first day I began. Then a chap I met in a bookstore put me on to mushrooms. I tell you, that made a difference right now. Mushrooms take you over the barrier when it comes to visions."

Asked how she prepared her potion, she laughed. "I don't. Not the bat's wing, gnat's eyelash potion. I don't believe in all that rigmarole of dancing and what not. It's time away from the real thing. The methodology of magic is lost. Concentration is the key to getting through to the spirits. As for the mushrooms, I sauté them with a banger [English slang for sausage] or put them in raw with my salad greens. They're rather good raw. They smell of the earth."

Eleanor Bone is pleased with the hard work the members of her coven are doing. Results can be felt in increased vibrations during the ceremonials. There are those who claim they have benefited from the coven's healing wish ritual.

A good beginner's exercise in concentration used by many of the witches is to think of a triangle. Rid the mind of all other thoughts and try to hold on to the image of the triangle for as long as possible. It sounds simple until it has been tried. Thoughts ranging from the most profound to the silliest crowd into the mind, pushing the triangle aside before one realizes what is going on. Regular practice can be exhausting.

Temper may have let one of the coven's success stories out of the bag. On overhearing a sly comment about the coven, one witch mentioned that they had revived an ancient method of controlling gossip. It requires a doll shaped to represent the gossip. A bit of the gossip's personal property hung on the doll helps. Then an incantation is chanted while the lips of the doll are carefully stitched together.

However, Eleanor Bone refuses to believe that blighting witchcraft of a serious nature is being practiced in England at this time. She claims that most of the stories that have hit the headlines as black magic are based on nothing more than pranks committed by bored school children. Witchcraft is hard work. No one is going to struggle through the process necessary to achieve genuine sorcery, white or black, for a joke.

There are those who say that to anger even a healing witch results in a curse. Lady Olwen Wilson, Curator of the Witchcraft Museum on the Isle of Man, is quite certain that Mrs. Bone herself was responsible for the heart attack Mrs. Wilson suffered following a dispute over the ownership of some museum displays.

In Somerset, the word witch implies black magic. A curing witch is called a charmer, a conjurer, or a wise one. One charming lady who lives in Somerset and is close to the world of magic is Miss Ruth Tongue. The co-author of *Folktales of England,* she is articulate about the craft if not about her personal involvement in it.

She points out that the moon goddess has several different aspects and a special name for each aspect. She is Cybele of the crescent moon; Selene of the full moon; and Pole Hechete of the waning or the dark of the moon. During the worst of the persecutions, when witches no longer dared to meet in the full of the moon, it became the custom to hold sabbats only during those times when the absence of moonlight helped conceal them. Naturally, at those times the moon goddess was addressed as Hecate and under that name came to be thought of popularly as a witch goddess.

In Somerset it is the old, remembered magic that is

practiced, not attempts to vivify book knowledge. Some of the ancient fertility dances are still performed in Abbots, Bromely, and Staffordshire, where male dance troops dressed in antler headdresses frolic and sing from village to village. Part of the reason magic has survived here is that Somerset enjoys a rural setting and has all the necessary accoutrements of magic.

Miss Tongue emphasizes the little-known power of the blacksmith in witchcraft. He works with iron and fire, both vital elements and power sources in themselves. He shapes the iron on an anvil, which is essentially an altar, so that his daily work is a worship in itself. If, in addition to this, the blacksmith has inherited ancient knowledge, he will be a gifted sorcerer. There is, for example, an incantation that can be uttered while a nail is shaped in a certain fashion to give it the power to lame a person if it is pounded into his footprint.

In the past, Somerset was famous for the ability of its witches in shape-shifting. In 1666, a female witch was hanged because she was caught, or so witnesses against her testified, in the act of changing into a rabbit. To commemorate her skill, today there is a cafe called The Lady & the Hare. There is another story of a Somerset boy who stood watching hounds and men on horseback chasing a fox. "Run, Granny," the boy screamed. A curious passer-by followed the boy home. At the doorway to their hut stood an old lady, panting and leaning against the side of the hut for support.

The local sorcerers were also adept at an enchantment made with a specially braided five-foot rope adorned at given intervals with feathers from a male goose. The "gander-feather ladder," as they called it, was used to summon people. Man or woman, young or old, willing or not, they came in response to the ladder.

Tradesmen-witches taking their wares to the fair performed the drawing-the-line spell. Once properly accomplished, no living creature could cross over the line until the spell was broken, unless the creature came walking from the opposite direction.

In Somerset no one will say whether sorcery is being practiced currently. Perhaps the hint came when Miss Tongue admitted that some folk in the countryside still keep toads closed up in boxes as familiars. It is also true that special notice is taken of a woman who is a Chimes child, one born between midnight on a Friday and cockcrow on Saturday. Such a person will grow up with a natural proclivity for healing sorcery. In England, where torture was not permitted during the old trials and the executions were fewer, more of the old religion may have survived than is seen on the surface. Now that the times are more permissive and the English atmosphere is growing favorable to witches, the next decade may see more and more evidence of the craft coming out of hiding.

If the trend continues, however, incidents of satanism will be among them.

In Westham Sussex not long ago, Mr. Walter Binstead, a bell-ringer for his local vicarage, spotted four suspicious-looking strangers entering the church. There was something about the quartet that suggested one man without aid would do well not to interfere. He managed to slip in close enough to see the four moving towards the altar and hear chanting in what sounded like a foreign language before going to call the authorities.

By the time the police arrived, the men were gone. However, they had left ample evidence of their activities. A quick look around his church convinced the Reverend Harold Coulthurst that he would have to research a ceremony not used by Anglican ministers for generations: the ritual of rehallowing the altar.

Evidently, the four men had singled out the eleventh-century Church of St. Mary the Virgin to make their attempt to communicate with evil spirits. Their deliberate acts of desecration convinced Reverend Coulthurst that the four men actually were in league with the Devil.

It looks as though that rehallowing ceremony will be only the first of many to be performed in English churches.

The Reverend J. L. Head, pastor of St. Clements at Leigh-on-the-Sea, Essex, was horrified to discover the heart of a recently killed sheep that had been ritually pierced with thirteen thorns before being placed on the grave of a woman he had reason to believe had been a witch. The mutilated heart was not intended to convey contempt, but had been placed on the witch's grave in a ritual performed by her peers to inter her bones properly and commemorate her death.

In Appleton, Berkshire, on All Souls' Eve, the headstones in a graveyard were overturned and marked with hex signs. An abandoned graveyard at St. Mary's Clophill in Gedforshire was defiled even more ominously. Six of its graves were broken into. From one grave, the bones of a woman were removed and used to mark off the familiar witch's circle. Authorities believe a Black Mass was conducted on the spot. And the authorities are beginning to wonder if the next step in the satanic movement will be a revival of ritual murder and cannibalism.

The number of incidents of desecration continues to grow. The level has now reached two hundred a year. However, some insist that this does not reflect a growth in the membership of the black magic cult, but simply a relaxation of wariness in its members or an increase in the level of hostility making wariness impossible.

More than a dozen years back, Robert Fabian, late of Scotland Yard, had reached this conclusion and published his warning in his memoirs. To substantiate his theory, he cited a number of incidents he had come across in his professional career. Among them was an account of a group of Pan worshippers who were luring young boys and girls into their circle to provide them with degrading public shows. A number of the Black Mass groups in London were offbeat; one of the covens had a distinct Parisian flavor. The members had imported a wooden fertility idol from Africa, whose most obvious protuberance their ecstatic rituals kept polished to a high, bright luster.

The sex sensationalists, with their compulsive flair for publicity, and the desecrationists, with their boneheaded lack of consideration for other people's sensibilities, are stirring up public wrath in England.

The laws making the practice of witchcraft illegal were wiped off the books in 1736 by an act of Parliament. Now voices are beginning to cry out that the laws against witchcraft should be restored. That, no doubt, was the reason Mrs. Bone was so vehement in her denial of the existence of satanism. It would be a great pity if the cones of power—the combined supernatural strength of individual covens—were to be destroyed just as they were beginning to grow again. For all the freaks and the foolish, angry people, England is better, the world is better for having the old cry ring out over English soil: "Listen to the words of the Great Mother who was of old called among men Artemis, Astarte, Dione, Melusine, Aphrodite, Cetedwen, Arianrod Bride, and by many other names."

CHAPTER ELEVEN

Hippie Witch

In America, the witches are young.

That is not absolutely true, of course. Some of the witchcraft being practiced at this moment is older than the white occupation of this continent. And some of the witches are older than one would think possible.

In the mountains of Tennessee and Kentucky, in the back country of Virginia and the Carolinas, there is a kind of magic that came to this country from the north of England, from the Highlands of Scotland, and from the black Irish. These people had learned about poverty and the cruelty of the rich, and they had come to mistrust strangers long before they crossed the Atlantic. Nothing their heirs have experienced on this side of the ocean has given them reason to soften that attitude.

Their forefathers had moved west steadily, generation by generation, always going farther because they did not like to be able to see their neighbors, even if it meant only a slim column of smoke rising from a distant cabin. They preferred silence to gossip, and hardship to interference.

Long before they set foot on these shores, the clans had developed the custom of fighting back when the government took too impertinent an interest in their affairs. Two hundred years later, the government is still getting its long nose tweaked when it pokes it into the mountain people's affairs.

These people still have not given up on the great Whiskey Rebellion of 1794. The federal government sent armed troops, thinking to cow the distillers, and when the open fighting stopped it thought the matter settled. Today, a brand of moonshine comes out of Tennessee as sweet and mellow as well water, and it takes off the top of your head like a blast from a twelve-gauge shotgun. Other regions dispute Tennessee's boast of superiority.

Compared to the way they feel about their witchcraft, the country people are forthright about the location of their stills. But witches are among them; and if you drink your booze in amiable silence, especially if you are good at making music and know a few good tunes, you will see them. Look and listen and nod your head. Come to your own conclusions, but do not meddle.

The new English covens chant and dance in their ceremonies to rhythm, but not to music. However, in the days when England was famous for her music, the saying went that the Devil had the best tunes. Those tunes are remembered and sung today in the southern Appalachians.

In fact, some conjurers say the tune is more important to an enchantment than the words. Every incantation contains power words, words that have no content but whose verbalization acts as a condenser of supernatural forces. To utter them frivolously is dangerous. A conjuring spell will contain three or four of these words. But a tune has no content at all; it is all power. They say a good tune can draw down and focus power the way a magnifying glass focuses the sun's rays.

In the mountains, they have healing magic. They have growing magic for the tobacco patches and their vegetable gardens. One man said that the Kentucky miners who were sneaking into old abandoned coal mines and digging out enough ore to keep their families from starving still had the old Welsh charms to keep the mine roof from caving in. He refused to name those who had the proper charms, but he said anyone could spot the men. They were the ones the other miners wanted to accompany into the mines.

"They don't like it none, though," he went on. "It's spell agin' spell. The earth doesn't hanker to be dug up. Mining leaves big, gaping holes in her sides. And some say there are little people in the earth who don't like it none, either.

"So the earth, and maybe the little people, too, are trying for a cave-in on the diggers' heads. The more diggers, the bigger the wrath. One man, say he has a charm his daddy taught him, it'll keep the dirt off his head. But you crowd in four or five extra without charms of their own, his charm isn't big enough for that.

"The men that own the charms, they go sneaking out in the early morning hours, sometimes before the first morning rays of sunshine, so as they can be alone. Those that get big-hearted and think to share what's theirs with neighbors don't last long. Sometimes their charms die with them. Leastwise, they say, there's fewer charms for the miners than there were in the old days."

Other kinds of conjuring magic have been lost when their owners have died before they could pass it along to the next generation. World War II, Korea, and Vietnam have taken a devastating toll; thousands of bachelors and husbands who were not yet fathers or were the fathers of infants never came back.

In most cases, once gone, the witchcraft is gone forever, for the big sabbats in which the witches come together to pick each other's brains and barter spells have no place in mountain magic. Crowds are conspicuous. And these close-mouthed people act on the assumption that the more people sharing a secret, the more likely one of them is to come down with a bad case of tongue-waggle.

Mountain magic is divided among the sexes. The spells, tunes, and recipes are passed on from father to son and from mother to daughter. When a woman has no daughter or her child dies, if she likes her daughter-in-law, she may pass on her knowledge that way. On the other hand, she may not. Many an old granny has died with set jaws, deaf to her family's wheedling to teach some of the conjuring power they know her to have.

The tunes are harder to keep private among these music-wise people. Bits of a tune will be overheard while the conjuration is in progress, or the tune will slip out in a whistle when the witch's mind is otherwise occupied. Without words, the conjuring tunes are undirected. Still, "The air has its own power and sometimes a tune will take a liking to it, squat down, and work just fine," a tenant farmer explained. "Nowadays, we go along with the power because half the time we're traveling blind."

One kind of magic still as widely known as in the old days are the spells and recipes related to moonshine. In fact, this kind of magic has increased as conjurations and tunes originally applied to other aspects of life have been put to use in keeping the local industry alive.

Having a common enemy has helped. The people would rather spite the government than be stingy with each other, hard feelings or no hard feelings. Drawing-the-line conjurations, hiding charms, and invisibility spells have been passed around even to non-relatives. Some comparative newcomers to the area, after they began taking part in the common sport and industry, have been told how to charm the smoke down so it hugs the ground, and what to sing if someone begins dogging their trail.

Yeast-growing songs, brewing mixtures, and brewing gods—small images to keep the fermenting mash from exploding in its containers—are traditional to the family. The efficiency of the magic can be determined by sampling the brew. Some families bottle a superior product. It is not the water, nor is it the aging or the barrels in which the whiskey is stored. Everyone wishes he owned the secret, but no one expects to learn it. That kind of secret, one has to be born to.

In the mountains, instead of the witch who is a general practitioner, coping with all the needs of the community, there are specialists. One family will oblige with water witching. Another has an old recipe for love potions. A third has good hunting magic, but it may be limited to a spell to help the dogs stay on scent. If you have bought a new rifle and need some words said over it to make it shoot true, you take it to some people who live thirty miles away.

There is more than a touch of satanism in the mountains. Curses and spells to lift them are not unknown. But the claim is that they shine especially in conjuring up spirits, demons, and the Devil himself. No one admits to doing it, though there are those who say they have seen it or heard it being done. There is no point in attempting to look for positive evidence. One thing is certain: the stories are believed in the mountains, and they have spells for quieting spirits and sending the Devil and his legions scampering back to hell to prove it. There is a saying in the coalfields of Kentucky that the miners live close enough to hell to make it a nice evening's walk for the Devil.

In the big cities like Chicago and New York, another kind of conjuring and cursing has filtered through the littered streets: voodoo. Black power has hit the headlines, but little is said about voodoo. This is not because it is not there on the surface for anyone to see, but because in this country we are conditioned not to take witchcraft seriously. To the reporters, voodoo is just a black superstition.

The brothers know differently. In any good-sized black community, shops sell charms, potions, and sacrificial vessels. In some neighborhoods, the shops feel free to display these wares in the window. These are the neighborhoods in which the live-chicken seller knows not all of his birds will reach the stewing kettle. Where pet stores carry a surprisingly heavy stock of snakes. Where the *hougan,* the voodoo priest, and the *mambo,* the priestess, are known to the local cop and are treated with respect.

Voodoo is no more universally accepted within the black community than Methodism is among whites. However, voodoo has the virtue of being entirely their bag. No matter where one begins to trace its antecedents, one ends up in Africa. No one in the community, not even an unbeliever, will inform on a voodoo priest. Even the university-educated black militants who do not believe in voodoo and care only about power politics and ghetto economics do not care to put down an institution that is part of the black heritage.

In recent years, attendance at the ritual has burgeoned along with the natural haircut, African-styled clothing, and Swahili. However, the real *hougans* and *mambos* are not black nationalists. Their interests are not national and economic, but local and personal. Mysticism and politics do not mix. It is unlikely that the nationalists will be able to develop a genuine priest-revolutionary, as is the avowed intention of some of the groups.

Voodoo may appear spontaneous and primitive to the uninitiated, but it is anything but that. A priest is born with some abilities and develops others as a result of effort so strenuous as to demand that it be his full-time occupation. Furthermore, voodoo is particularly demanding among types of sorcery. Much of its power comes from possession. This is an aspect of witchcraft that is not within the compass of this book. One basic characteristic of possession, accepted by all who have utilized it, including Greek oracles, Aztec priests, Eskimo shamans, and Miami spiritualist mediums, is that the experience drains the one possessed. Immediately after the possession and into the next day, often into the following week, the person is weak and ill. In voodoo, the spirits, the *loa,* not only take over a priest's voice, they seize the entire body and make it gyrate wildly. The sessions often last for hours.

Voodoo has lost little of its strength since it left its ancestral home. Reports insist that a *hougan* can work spells to recall the dead as zombies, turn back bullets, and repel or summon evil spirits. No wonder the black militants are trying to recruit a priest.

However, the entire life of a priest is oriented toward the spirit world. To maintain and increase that contact is his life's work. The focus of a military leader is outward. The two disciplines are not congruent. The best the black militants can hope for in the way of a voodoo leader is a quasi-priest, one who has had some experience and has tried for rapport with the supernatural world, but has essentially failed. A reject.

Using such an individual in the movement is not without merit. It would be rather like a pharmaceutical house hiring a medical school drop-out to sell its products. At least he would be acquainted with the doctor's vocabulary. A voodoo reject would know the language and be familiar with the problems a priest must cope with. He would have a feeling for the ways in which voodoo could be useful to the movement and the ways in which the two groups could not come together.

New York, Florida, Los Angeles, and other areas where the Cubans fleeing Castro have settled are acquiring *curanderos* and *brujos* of a slightly different kind than the Mexican-American sorcerers. More fortunate than many of the refugees, the *curanderos* have a profession that has transplanted well. Certainly, they have received no competition from the Mexican-American professionals. There is great national snobbery among Spanish-speaking peoples. They cannot tolerate each other's accents; they despise each other's foods; and they would rather be sick than be attended by each other's *curanderos*.

The healers who came ashore in Miami were as ragged and empty-handed as their fellow refugees. However, they immediately set up shop, first practicing out of their barrack-like quarters, then out of their two-room apartments, then from their homes, and finally, in some cases, from well-appointed offices. In the beginning, they charged nothing or bartered their services, for such money as a family had was needed to buy food for hungry mouths. The *Cubanos* are a proud people. Those who found jobs remembered past favors and paid their obligations.

An effort was made for the purposes of this book to determine whether blighting magic was being used in the political conflict in Cuba. If there are *curanderos*, it stands to reason that there are also blighting witches. However, no discussion on this issue was permitted. No one hinted. No one winked or smiled. Heavy silence greeted leading questions, and when the conversation was taken up again, the topic had been changed.

Strict secrecy about the broader outlines of witchcraft is not typical of New World witchcraft in Spanish-speaking countries. The critical factor operating here is probably political. There is always the possibility that some freakish accident has destroyed blighting witchcraft in Cuba; the silences may have sprung from embarrassment. But the likelihood seems small. One day, when the internecine conflict is over and travel to and from Cuba is open, when tongues are no longer guarded, the answer will come out.

There is nothing guarded about Puerto Rican blighting sorcery, as the law firm for which President Nixon formerly worked recently discovered to its horror. The firm represents the General Cigar Company, whose product is manufactured on the island. The International Association of Machinists and Aerospace Workers has been trying to persuade the men who make the cigars to unionize in order to obtain a lever in their fight for better pay and working conditions. As one might expect, the company has resisted the effort, utilizing its capacity to exert subtle and not-so-subtle pressure.

Since the standard of living and the employment picture on the island were poor, the company did not anticipate failure. However, failure was what it found. And it was its move to recoup its losses that placed the law firm in the awkward position of requesting the National Labor Relations Board to adjudge the collective bargaining election null and void on the grounds that the union had used unfair tactics—to wit, sorcery.

The company, through its law firm, asserts that one of the employees hired a witch for $150 a week to apply her *brujeria,* her witchcraft, to the union cause. Another worker bought a magic potion which had the property of preventing those who smelled it from voting against the union. According to the company, the *brujeria* was so successful that at the time of the election, (1) workers who had intended to vote for the company felt physically ill; (2) workers were unable to see on the ballot the box marked "no union"; (3) workers could not remember afterwards whether they had voted for or against the company; and (4) many workers were not able to attend the election because while it was being held, the sky fell apart and poured down gallons of shot-sized drops driven by gale-velocity winds. As soon as the election was over, the rain dried up, the wind died down, and the sun sparkled in a jay-bird-blue sky.

The fiftieth state of the union also has its own magic that came to the islands over open reaches of the Pacific in tiny outrigger canoes. The Polynesians who made the journey felt that they would never have reached the islands without sorcery. Contemporary navigators who have considered their feat are inclined to agree with them.

Their most vital technology was magic. Even the design and construction of their ocean-going canoes was accomplished through the use of special "power" tools by men who were known to have ship-building magic in their fingertips. The entire project was kept under the watchful gaze of well-propitiated spirits. The navigators were chosen in a similar fashion. Every aspect of the voyage was supported by supernatural help. Once the Polynesians had located their final homes and begun the generations-long task of settling in, the skills their new way of life required were developed as cooperative ventures between the world of men and the realm of the supernatural.

When white men introduced disease, filth, poverty, and guilt into one of the happiest, healthiest cultures the world has ever known, they tricked the Polynesians into trading their working magic for the impressive appearance of the products of their own materialistic culture. They shamed the sleek brown bodies into tents of cheap cotton cloth. They drove apart man and woman with the concept of sin and nastiness.

Today, increasing numbers of Polynesians and their mixed descendants—the white men indulged the flesh even as they vilified it—have realized the value of what they gave up. In the isolated areas of the islands, the ancient *Kahuna* sorcery had lingered on. Now it is spreading once again. Some of the old arts have been lost; others are no longer needed.

As long as children are born and people quarrel, healing and blighting magic will be called upon. Dr. Harold M. Johnson, a physician in Honolulu, has had personal experience with the effectiveness of Hawaiian blighting sorcery, *Kahua Anaana*. He has written up cases of patients who died after being cursed, despite the best efforts of modern medicine. He has observed formerly healthy skin crust over and break open in raw cracks in response to a *Kahuna*'s order.

Fishing magic is another branch of sorcery that is still being practiced. The Hawaiians do their serious fishing in the dark of night, standing up in their outriggers, holding a flaming torch in one hand and a spear in the other. The torch attracts fish to the surface of the water, and the spear brings them into the outrigger. Even during the period of their strongest influence, the missionaries were never able to wipe out fishing magic. The food for a man's family and the man's life itself depended on it. The outrigger, the spear, the torch, and the expedition, each has its own particular spell.

In recent years, some of the wealthier Hawaiians have gone modern, giving up the old ways of night fishing for motor boats and battery-operated electric lanterns. For a while, the modernists had poor results to show for their expenditure. Then one boat in the fleet began coming in loaded down with fish. The other owners pestered him for the secret of what he was doing, but they could not pry a word out of him. Finally, his friends began giving him the cold shoulder. An old-time buddy told him that the anger was growing dangerous: some of the men were talking *Kahua Anaana*. The boat owner looked embarrassed. He blurted out, "All I've been doing is going back to saying the old spells again."

Unlike the Hawaiians, the descendants of the Germans who settled stretches of the Midwest have lost most of their working magic. Public education, radio, magazines, newspapers, and television have done a thorough job on them. Growing charms and cooking spells have gone the way of home vegetable gardens, home-cured sauerkraut, and hand-stuffed sausages.

But a few grannies are left who can dry the milk in a cow's udder or make a pig tear out of his pen in a frenzy. One story is circulating around the farm country of Pennsylvania about a sweet little old lady who gave a bunch of young fellows from Columbia University the scare of their lives. The fellows were on motorcycles, and the noise the bikes were making as they roared up and down the country road was keeping her hens from laying. She asked them politely to find another road for their drag racing. Then she asked them less politely. Then they sassed her. She disappeared for a while after that. Then, the fellows later claimed, a crack of thunder and a splat of jagged light with a presence in the middle came streaking out of the old lady's house. They did not know what it was, and they did not stay around to investigate.

The little old lady told her neighbors: "I couldn't reason with them. So I asked a friend of mine to help me out. Looks like he reasoned with them real good."

Valuable as they are and as they have been to our heritage, in one way or another all the Yankee witches that have been discussed in this section are hand-me-downs from other cultures. But a true native form has sprung up in the last decade, mutated, bewildering, unruly, charged with vitality, plagued with lack of discipline, and loaded with charm: the hippie witch.

In this context, the word hippie indicates only individuality in personal attire, coiffure, decor, and decorum. Hippie witches have been found among bank employees, civil servants, social workers, patrol officers, college students, nomads, lawyers, interns, shop owners, musicians, motion picture producers, directors, and actors, and investment firm trainees. Our census lacked the necessary funds for thoroughness, and without question this list is incomplete.

These mutant witches are pragmatic in the extreme and anti-dogma in principle. Some attach themselves to established religions: Christianity (three male witches have become Doctors of Divinity and have opened their own church), Hinduism, Buddhism, and Mohammedanism. But hundreds of witches spit at the mention of religion, throwing their evangelical fervor into politics and social reform. Or music. Or art. Or science. Or sex. Or new patterns of living, such as communes or line marriage. They are nothing if not eclectic. It is true that these interests are being explored by others without the quickening influence of witchery. However, the practice of magic and interest in the supernatural grow daily.

Most of the new witches are antithetical to organization. The practice of sorcery spreads among them like the influenza virus, from person to person. There is no initiation, no apprenticeship—only, "Hey man, I got a way for doing that. Let me lay it on you." And a conjuration or a recipe is passed along.

The old magic is used when it is known. New magic is also being made. One anthropology student recites this charm before climbing into her car:

>Rubber,
>Rubber,
>Watch over me.
>Take care of me,
>Both me and my car.
>
>Yes, I accelerate,
>I drive down freeways,
>I dodge through traffic;
>
>Reckless drivers,
>Blind drivers,
>Stupid drivers

> Would injure me,
> Would crash into me,
> Would cut me down.
>
> I am made of flesh and bones.
> As for you,
> Spirit of the automobile,
> Spirit of rubber,
> Spirit of gleaming metal,
>
> Let loose your strength
> And fend off my foes.

Conflict with authorities over issues ranging from drug use to permissible length of hair are turning numbers of the new witches on to blighting sorcery.

There is no question that a majority of these witches take drugs or that the drugs they take put them in violation of federal and state laws. They claim their drug-taking is a vital part of their religious practice and the laws put them in the same position as that of Catholic priests celebrating the mass during prohibition. Responsible liberal leaders point out that the label of religion could be seized upon by hundreds of drug-takers who have nothing more disciplined in mind than a party, even while acknowledging that, properly used, the hallucinogenics have produced valuable results. Conservatives refuse to admit any conceivable benefit in using any drugs other than brain-damaging alcohol and cancer-producing tobacco.

Most conjuring of discomfort for the authorities is done by individuals after personal encounters with various segments of the establishment, but some of the hostility is beginning to clot into groups. The Women's International Terrorist Corps from Hell, known breath-savingly as WITCH, invaded the Social Science

Building of the University of Chicago not long ago to fling a curse on an opponent: "Fie on thee, Morris Janowitz! A hex on thy strategy!" And a Catholic university uncovered a coven of warlocks whose sorcery was more sinister and more secret.

More often, antagonism generated by opposing viewpoints drains off in practical jokes. A sorcery-oriented commune whose members knew they were being watched by the Narco squad for possible drug violations recently, with apparent secrecy and much to-do, hiked five miles up a rugged canyon and put together two long, narrow garden plots lining the stream bed that was the canyon's floor. When the naturally-watered plants were about two feet tall, the expected raid took place. To the commune's collective delight and the police department's subsequent embarrassment, two squad cars pulled up to the mouth of the canyon. Six officers carrying shovels and boxes dirtied their shoes and wet their foreheads climbing up to destroy the garden and carry down copious samples of what proved on close examination to be not *Cannabis sativa,* the hemp plant whose seeds and leaves yield marijuana, but thriving cuttings of *Sambucus,* the elder tree that traditionally grows wherever witches live.

The noise and frivolity of the new witches offends many of the traditionalists. Last year in northern California, a usually amiable Irish lady, highly skilled in healing sorcery for both humans and animals, refused for a time to have anything to do with a group of young witches who had traveled from the campus of the University of California at Santa Cruz especially to see her. Finally, one of the girls in the group was able to get close enough to her to ask why she was snubbing them.

"Look at you," the Irish witch grumbled, pointing at her see-through blouse. "Half naked and no better than you should be, I don't doubt, traipsing about with men and sleeping God knows where. You would be a disgrace to the calling."

The girl grinned and said impudently, "I'll bet you were too when you were my age. Witches are always a disgrace to their calling. That's their thing. It's the power simmering in us."

It was the beginning of a friendship.

The new witches are not afraid of public attention. Attention is congruent with their aim of creating a new climate of opinion. They want to counteract the technocracy of our culture and emphasize life consciousness. They want the whole country to go supernatural. One prophet, whose material possessions consist of a motorcycle, a knapsack, and a passenger-companion cat, said seriously, "Everyone, even the squares, even the pigs, need to have magic in their lives."

To this end, they welcome publicity as an avenue of teaching. They open up to comparative strangers. They tend to be tolerant of divergent paths and the eccentricities of others. One girl said, "Even a nowhere witch is better than no witch at all. In a country that spends more money on cosmetics than feeding starving babies, you can't afford to be fussy."

Contacting traditional witches is largely a matter of luck, and generally the luck is bad. Finding the new witches is relatively simple. The underground newspapers often carry news of them in their regular columns or advertisements inviting those with similar interests to get together for a rap session. Proprietors of head shops that carry a heavy stock of supernatural items may know who is who, and proprietors of occult book shops will often know a few witches. If they refuse to talk, it is safe to conclude they are of the old school.

High school, college, and university night schools are beginning to form classes that study witchcraft. Check the school papers and night school schedules of classes.

Many neighborhood community centers oriented towards young people are also studying witchcraft. Ask one of the directors.

There is a Six-Day School in Sonoma, California that is directed to the study of the supernatural.

Many of the sensitivity-training groups are oriented toward developing psychic powers. Ask around.

A national Druid organization exists with many local branches. Check your local phone book.

In San Francisco, California, Halloween 1969 will be celebrated by the opening of a Temple of Cannabis dedicated to mystically oriented religious ceremonies in which cannabis will be used as a sacrament.

Classified advertisements in daily newspapers may contain veiled invitations. Look for such words as "Old Religion," "Pagan," and "Sacred."

If all available sources in this country fail, try writing to Lady Olwen Wilson, Curator of the Witchcraft Museum, Isle of Man. She has offered to answer all responsible inquiries about witchcraft.

Don't wait for a reply. Make a start now.

CHAPTER TWELVE

Beginnings

The stimulus behind this book is hope.

All the signs say the last third of this century will be favorable to witchcraft. Mystics report an improvement in vibrations. Some of the underground stirrings have even hit the headlines.

Political and social commentators tell us we are on the brink of revolution. They point to the tension between the races, between the haves and the have-nots, between the extremes of the political left and right, between the young and the old. They point to the violence that has touched every level of our society. They point to draft-card burning, to the drug scene, to the mass dropout of middle class youth from the prosperity and regimentation their parents have arranged for them, to the accumulation of weapons at both ends of the political scale.

And having pointed, they lament. The revolution they expect is one of blood and broken heads and rioting in the streets. It has not occurred to them that the revolution may be of a different nature. It may be a revolution of the spirit against the rationalistic, object-loving, power-abusing environment in which we find ourselves. The end of that revolution would be a diminution of violence and a channeling of energy into creative enterprises.

The violence that has erupted through the rigid structure built by the middle class in this country has been a boil-off of spirit, contained, suppressed, and squeezed until the pressure became unendurable.

Freedom of the individual rests on freedom of spirit. Repression of spirit is the foundation for all other kinds of slavery. As a rule, the prophets of religion have fought for freedom. They have preached freedom. They have practiced freedom. They have created an aura of freedom. To be close to them was to become free. But too often the followers of the prophets obsessively insist in the name of the prophet that only one narrow path in life is permissible for all of mankind. They attempt to destroy all other paths, and in the process destroy the freedom that allows the spirit to thrive.

The growth of materialism in the eighteenth and nineteenth centuries in the Western world was a reaction against this kind of repression. The reaction was good. Many of the products of the reaction were also good. Exploration and control over the material world is an exciting, vital facet of human capability.

It is not, however, the only facet that needs developing.

The prophets of materialism have become as rigid and repressive in their turn as all the others before them. In the name of their new religion, they have burned books, attacked temples of learning, and ridiculed, hounded, and persecuted those who will not worship at their shrines.

In the 1920s, another bloodless revolution erupted in

this country. It was the sexual revolution, which was interrupted first by the depression of the thirties and then by the holocaust of the forties and is only now coming to fruition. Although the sexual revolution manifested itself most prominently in behavior, its impetus can be found in the attempts of spirit to escape from the prison-house of pretense.

Over-impressed with the accomplishments of materialism, the people of the Western world took on nature. Man would conquer nature and twist her to his own devices. In consonance with that goal, he began to deny his own nature. He tried to ignore his animal heritage and to live like his concept of an angel. Any reminder of his true nature was sufficient to send him into a rage. So began an era of formality and hypocrisy that warped social relationships and individual personality.

As part of this program, sexuality has been beleaguered almost beyond belief. For generations, the processes that bring forth new life have been denounced as nasty and shameful; the body that houses the human spirit has been called disgusting. These attitudes were shaped by social conditioning methods so effective that millions of men and women have lived and died with their sexual feelings deadened or distorted beyond recognition.

Sexuality is man's strong instinctual tie to nature in a world that is increasingly locking us away from organic life in concrete, steel, and asphalt jungles. The heat and rhythm of sexuality have a vital influence on the entire range of human emotion.

The sexual revolt of the sixties is, in fact, an emotional revolt. For generations, the proponents of rationalism have denied that there is any valid place in human planning for emotion. Emotions have been relegated to moments of private entertainment, and even there they are accepted with a certain amount of embarrassment. Important matters like international politics and national welfare must be conducted dispassionately according to programs free of emotional taint. The result of this policy has been to enmesh the Western world in programs that are antithetical to happiness, sanity, and life itself.

Ironically, if one questions these same anti-emotionalists as to the wisdom of their conclusions, they resort to hysterical name-calling and terrorist tactics. All of this suggests that reason does not rule emotion. And if this is the case, persisting in the attempt to achieve a social structure dominated by rationalism is not only futile but dangerous.

Emotions and reason exist side by side within the human psyche, and both must participate in the process of organizing human life. For effective participation, emotions need to be strengthened and developed, not repressed. The problem has been the difficulty of making a beginning in a society in which the smallest display of spontaneous emotion is likely to meet hostility. Sex has been deliberately exploited toward this end because its strong instinctual force has been able to stir long-deadened emotions.

The sexual rebels of the twenties seemed only to be escaping from the boredom of a repressed life. It is a hopeful sign that today's sexual rebels show promise of striving for more. They are endeavoring to bring their lives once more into harmony with nature. There are no signposts along the way, and they make mistakes. Of taste. Of discretion. Of health. But they are showing a willingness to learn from their mistakes. The life they are demanding for themselves is one of greater sensuality, greater freedom of emotion honestly expressed, greater freedom of body movement; this has already pushed them out-of-doors, out of the plaster cocoons in which their parents spent so much of their lives, into the sunshine, closer to other life forms.

There is hope that this movement will go beyond a struggle for emotional freedom and try to revive the natural mysticism that has been even more viciously repressed than man's emotional nature.

Peculiarly enough, the group leader of this new movement is the late George Bernard Shaw. As early as 1924, he was complaining that science had replaced Christianity in the role of theological tyrant. He suggested that the ingestion of a wafer in the belief it would further spiritual salvation might be less superstitious and less harmful than the unquestioned handing over of one's being to the mercies of a legion of medical specialists, each of whom is eager to take his specialized, expensive whack at it. He warned against our unquestioning faith in science and "our deafness and blindness to the calls and visions of the inexorable power that made us, and will destroy us if we disregard it."

The shrewdness of Shaw's remarks is becoming increasingly apparent to young people. The feeling is growing among them that science has failed. Signs painted on fences read *Science is a cop-out*.

One sophomore enrolled in the Physics Department at Columbia is spending more and more of his time teaching music and dance to Puerto Rican pre-schoolers. He said, pointing to the children, "The future starts here, not in the laboratory. Science demands that we believe in nothing that is not amenable to observation and measurement. There is more to man than that which can be observed and measured."

Students disgusted with the smug stagnation of

church religion have shouted, "God is dead"; now other students, disillusioned with the failure of the rationalists, are crying, "Science is dead!"

It is true that the rebellion against rationalism is a movement of young people. It is also true that representatives of every age level swell its numbers. The young, because of their exuberance and the greater time at their disposal, are more apparent in the movement. But they are not alone. The movement was waiting for them when they were ready for it; the movement was there before they were born. And those who are responsible for its being there are valued friends, fellow-rebels, and teachers.

This revolution cannot be written off as a product of the generation gap. It is a revolution of the spirit. As don Juan pointed out, for those who engage in the life of the spirit, to give in to old age is to be crushed and defeated. This movement welcomes maturity that has not lost the capacity to fight. One artist, living in a tree house on the Red Star Ranch in Sonoma, commented, "The years bring wisdom and that's what it's all about, but senescence is a bummer."

It is. Hardening of ideas and attitudes is worse than hardening of the arteries. And both diseases can strike any age group.

Just as reason and emotion function best when they are working together, so each age level functions best in an environment that appreciates and utilizes its special properties. The failure of our present social system to produce such an environment is only one of its many obvious weaknesses. Not only is our culture tearing along in a manner disagreeable and unfulfilling to many of the individuals who are forced to live in it, but its collective greed and stupidity are destroying the physical environment in which it exists. The atmosphere we breathe, the streams, oceans, lakes, and soil are swiftly being made unfit for human life. And still another threat hangs over our lives daily: we live in a world in which a single error in a few men's judgment could result in a cataclysm that will render it incapable of sustaining any kind of life at all.

The need for magic is critical.

Not all the people currently exploring the strange world of the metaphysical do so with conviction, or even with much hope for success. A graduate student in history at Stanford University recently joined a coven, confessing to her friends, "I don't really believe in witchcraft. However, one thing I know from my studies. We've tried all the avenues of non-magic and they have failed us. It's time to try something new." A physicist working for an internationally known research organization, who has been an active member of a coven for more than a year, also has difficulties in the area of belief. Shaking his head wryly, he said, "Often part way through a ceremony I find myself wondering, 'What am I doing here?' and I can feel myself growing red for being so foolish, but I finish the ceremony and next month I try again."

Time is what we are running short of. On the one hand, we are breeding ourselves out of standing room; and on the other, we are steadily destroying the resources we have left with our own filth.

It would seem that the time has come to return to the beliefs of those first men who struggled for survival on a savage but unspoiled planet—that nature is sacred, and that it is up to man to arrange his affairs in harmony with her, for failure to do so will inevitably result in disaster. They perceived and respected the individuality of the other living beings with whom they shared the planet. Intuitively, they understood what we have learned through the use of microscopes: that even so-called inanimate objects vibrate with molecular motion that has its own unique organization. We have attempted to exploit the information. They used it to reinforce their sense of kinship with the mountains and streams, the ocean and soil, and the tools that were a part of their lives.

A sense of the sacred is perhaps the key difference between witches and rationalists.

Rationalists have seized their power contemptuously from nature, glorying in their own strength and knowledge, attempting to force more from nature than she is ready to give. Contempt has made them overconfident and tricked them into believing they are greater than the forces that shaped the universe. The pervasive atmosphere of contempt has poisoned their attitudes toward their fellow men and toward themselves.

Witches have obtained their powers from nature reverently and with awe. They are cautious and they teach their followers to be cautious, careful always to give back something of value in exchange for what they receive. They never forget their relationship with the world around them. They never forget that the universe is larger than their own ability to comprehend. Wonder, the sense of what is sacred, lights up their lives and teaches them that man who sprang from nature is filled with a dignity of his own. In the long run, that perception may be a witch's most important power.

For the Millions Series

FM-1 An Astrology Primer
FM-2 E. S. P.
FM-3 A Supernatural Primer
FM-4 Psychic Self-Improvement
FM-5 An Occult Dictionary
FM-6 Famous Ghosts, Phantoms, and Poltergeists
FM-7 Borderline Oddities
FM-8 Handwriting Analysis
FM-9 Miracle Cures
FM-10 Haunted Houses
FM-11 U. F. O.s
FM-12 Mental Telepathy and E. S. P. Powers
FM-13 Reincarnation
FM-14 Spirit Communication
FM-15 Tarot
FM-16 Seances and Sensitives
FM-17 Out-of-Body Experiences
FM-18 Phrenology
FM-19 Understanding Dreams
FM-20 Prophecy
FM-21 Hypnotism
FM-22 Spiritual Yoga
FM-23 Psychic Talents
FM-24 More E. S. P.
FM-25 Developing E. S. P.
FM-26 Dowsing, Waterwitches, and Divining Rods
FM-27 Lost Continents
FM-28 Unity
FM-29 Complete I Ching
FM-30 Scientology
FM-31 Secret Psychic Organizations
FM-32 Secrets of Egypt
FM-33 Witchcraft
FM-34 Understanding Zen

FM-35 MORE TAROT SECRETS
FM-36 COMPLETE HAND READING
FM-37 CHARMS, SPELLS, AND CURSES
FM-38 VEDANTA
FM-39 SCIENCE OF MIND
FM-40 AMERICAN INDIAN RELIGIONS
FM-41 VOODOO
FM-42 NUMEROLOGY
FM-43 THEOSOPHY
FM-44 CONVERSATIONS WITH THE BEYOND
FM-45 UNDERSTANDING JUNG
FM-46 WEREWOLVES, SHAPESHIFTERS, AND SKINWALKERS
FM-47 ALCHEMY
FM-48 UNDERSTANDING THE KABBALAH